책속 음원
바로 듣기!

음원 듣기 & 온라인 단어 학습

남다른 학습법으로
기적 같은 실력을 보장하는

기적의 영어리딩

체계적인 6단계 커리큘럼

	1 with 파닉스	2 with 주제 어휘	3 with 문장 패턴
목표	큰소리 리딩으로 문자 해독력을 높여요	리딩의 재미를 알며 기초 어휘력을 쌓아요	필수 문형을 접하며 문장 이해력을 높여요
리딩 소스	일상 이야기, 만화, 동화, 서사 논픽션 읽기	일상 이야기, 만화, 동화, 서사 논픽션 읽기	초대장, 포스터, 규칙 등의 정보·지식이 결합된 스토리 읽기
난이도	AR 0.5~1.0 Lexile BR~50 Words 50~70 (6p)	AR 0.7~1.5 Lexile 25~200 Words 70~90 (6p)	AR 1.3~2.3 Lexile 125~400 Words 90~110 (4p)
성취 수준	기초 어휘 180개	초등 3~4학년 교과서 수준 필수 어휘 180개	초등 5~6학년 교과서 수준 필수 어휘 200개

✓ 독해력 성장의 핵심 과정을 탄탄하게 밟아가는 6단계 리딩 프로그램

✓ 기적만의 3-Step 완전학습 시스템으로 확실한 학습 성과를 보장!

✓ 새 교육과정을 연계한 콘텐츠로 리딩 기초부터 중학 수준까지 저절로 완성!

✓ 적정 학습분량과 친절한 학습안내로 혼자서도 끝까지 완주 가능

4 with 문장 구조	5 with 문법	6 with 서술형 영작
다양한 글감을 읽으며 문장 구성력을 키워요	글을 논리적으로 이해하여 핵심을 파악해요	읽은 내용을 바탕으로 정리하는 표현력을 길러요
일상 소재의 실용문, 짧은 논픽션 읽기	교과 연계된 최신 소재의 정보글 읽기	교과 연계된 최신 소재의 정보글, 의견글 읽기
AR 2.3~3.3 Lexile 420~620 Words 100~130	AR 3.0~3.9 Lexile 550~680 Words 130~150	AR 3.7~4.7 Lexile 650~780 Words 150~180
고학년 독해력 완성	예비중 리딩·문법 통합	중학 독해·서술형 시험 대비

리딩 첫 시작부터 독해력 완성까지!

기본 다지기 — 영어와 친해지는 스토리 리딩으로 기본 바탕을 튼튼히!

Level 1 Level 2 Level 3

기적의 영어리딩 Level 1~3

- 초등 저학년의 영어 성장을 위한 리딩 기초 학습서
- 일상 이야기, 카툰, 동화 등 흥미로운 스토리로 리딩을 즐겁게 시작
- 따라가면 저절로 학습이 완성되는 3-STEP(읽기-이해-확장) 매일 학습
- 리딩의 기본기를 탄탄히 하는 파닉스 → 어휘 → 문장을 순차적으로 강화

실력 완성하기 — 논픽션 리딩으로 읽고 이해하고 표현하는 힘 기르기!

기적의 영어리딩 Level 4~6

- 초등 고학년의 문해력 완성과 중학 영어로의 연결을 돕는 리딩 심화 학습서
- 다양한 실용문과 정보글을 읽으며 글의 구조를 시각화하고 핵심을 파악하는 힘 강화
- 읽은 내용을 바탕으로 정리하고 표현하는 서술형 영작 훈련
- 문장 구조 → 논리적 이해 → 표현력 확장으로 이어지는 단계별 아웃풋 설계

3B

90~110 words
AR 1.3~2.3

기적의 영어리딩

with 문장 패턴

길벗스쿨

기적만의

3-Step 완전학습 시스템

읽고, 이해하고, 확장하는 3-Step 시스템으로 겉핥기가 아닌 진짜 실력을 키웁니다. 하나의 지문을 3단계에 걸쳐 깊이 있게 학습하면서 콘텐츠를 제대로 소화합니다. 동시에, 리딩의 기본 바탕이 되는 파닉스-어휘력-문장력을 차례로 강화합니다. 단순한 읽기를 넘어 문해력 성장을 위한 핵심 학습이 통합적으로 이루어지는 학습법입니다.

Step 1. 읽기

단어 익히기

지문을 이해하는 데 필수적인 키워드를 먼저 학습합니다.

스토리 리딩

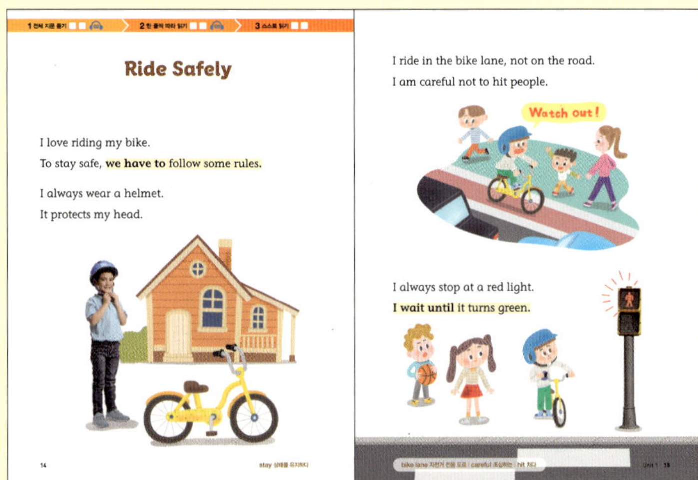

생활 속 규칙과 사회·문화 지식을 담은 이야기를 반복해서 듣고 읽으며 단어와 표현을 쉽게 체화합니다.

Step 2. 이해

내용 확인 문제

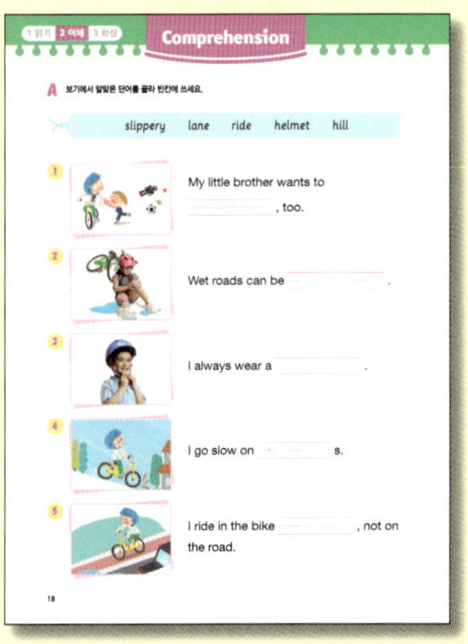

다양한 유형의 문제를 통해 읽은 내용을 충분히 이해하고, 단어 및 문장을 반복 학습하게 됩니다.

Step 3. 확장

필수 문형 학습

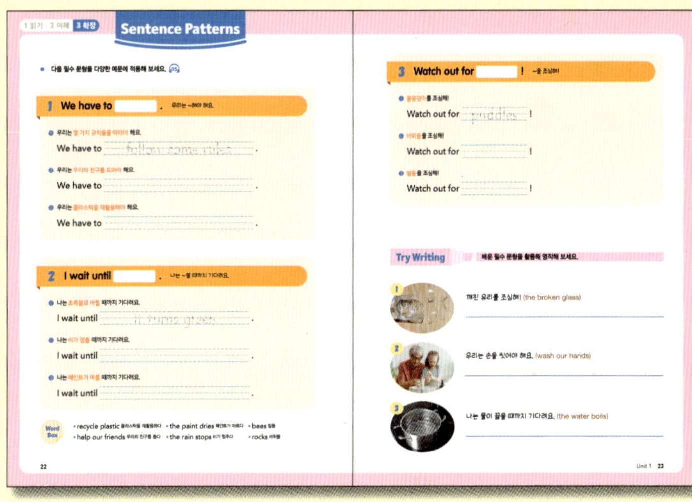

실력을 한 단계 더 끌어올리는 핵심학습을 짚고 갑니다.
Level 3에서는 문장 이해력을 높이는 필수 문형을 익히고 활용합니다.

Contents

Level 3B

How to Study

정보 · 지식이 담긴 흥미로운 스토리를 읽으며 문장 이해에 필수적인 다양한 문형을 익힙니다.

Level 3은 생활 속 규범, 사회 · 과학 지식이 결합된 이야기 지문으로 구성되어 있습니다. 흥미롭고 실용적인 이야기와 더불어 초대장 · 안내문 · 포스터 · 표 등 다양한 시각적 자료를 함께 접하며 읽고 이해하는 힘을 기릅니다.

또한 자주 쓰이는 교과서 필수 문형을 집중 학습합니다. 문형에 익숙해지면 리딩 속도와 이해력이 향상되고, 라이팅 활용 능력도 자연스럽게 길러집니다.

Step 1. 읽기

주요 단어를 익힌 다음 지문 따라 읽기

❶ **[Key Words]**에서 지문 이해에 중요한 단서가 되는 핵심 단어를 확인해요.

❷ **[온라인 단어 학습]**에서 단어를 반복 학습하며 뜻과 철자를 꼼꼼하게 익혀요.

❸ 간단한 문제를 풀며 단어를 잘 익혔는지 확인해요.

❹ 두 가지 버전의 음원을 잘 듣고 따라 읽어요.

- **[전체 지문 듣기]** 이야기를 잘 들으며 어떤 내용인지 파악해 보세요.
- **[한 줄씩 따라 읽기]** 한 문장씩 듣고 따라 읽어 보세요.
- **[스스로 읽기]** 처음부터 끝까지 정확하게 읽어 보세요.

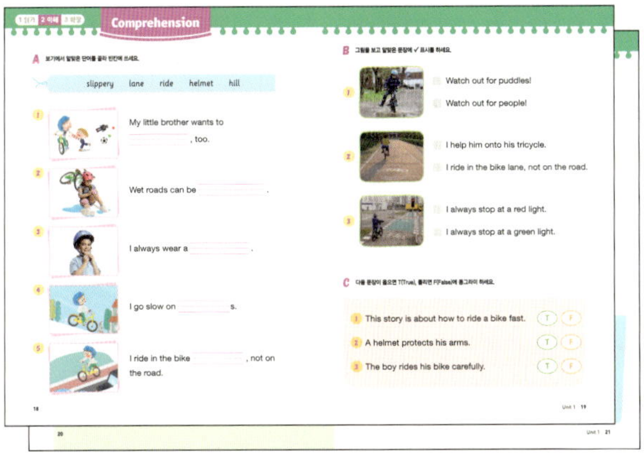

Step 2. 이해

문제를 풀며 지문을 제대로 이해하기

❶ [Comprehension]에서 여러 유형의 문제를 풀며 지문 이해도를 확인해요. 읽은 내용 정리하기, 반복 듣기, 생각 표현하기 코너를 통해 단어와 표현을 다지고 사고력도 함께 키워요.

❷ 문제 풀이 후 **[별책]** 정답지를 참고하여 채점하고 틀린 문제를 확인해 보세요.

Step 3. 확장

꼭 알아야 할 필수 문장패턴 익히기

❶ [Sentence Patterns]에서 필수 문형을 익히고 다양한 예문을 통해 연습해요.

❷ 배운 문형을 활용해 [Try Writing]에서 영작 연습을 해요.

❸ [Think More]에서 지문의 이야기 주제와 관련하여 한 발 더 나아간 액티비티를 풀며 다양한 정보와 지식을 탐구하고 관련 영어 표현을 익혀요.

[Review Test]

리뷰 테스트 2회분이 포함됩니다. Unit 1~4 테스트, Unit 5~8 테스트로 실력을 확인해 보세요.

[별책: Practice Book]

스토리 속 문장을 의미 단위로 나누어 읽고 직접 써 보면서 문장 감각을 키우는 연습을 합니다.

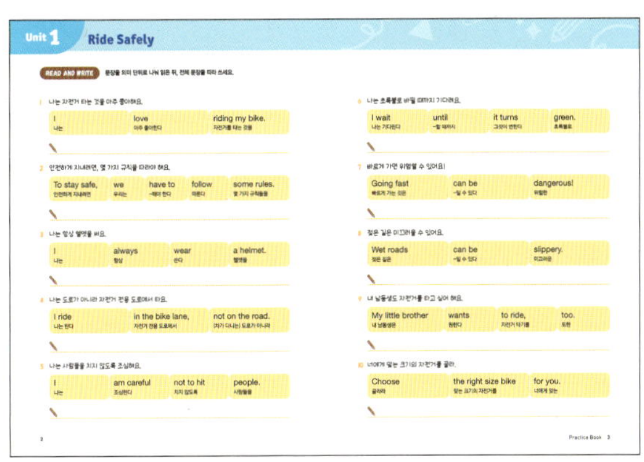

Study Plan

학습 완주를 위해 미리 학습계획을 세워 보세요.
26일 동안 집중하는 한 달 완성하기, 또는 주 3일 학습으로 차근차근 8주 완성하기!
나에게 맞는 방법을 정하고 진도표를 따라 끝까지 공부해 보세요.

26일 완성 학습 스케줄

Unit 1			Unit 2		
1. 읽기	2. 이해	3. 확장	1. 읽기	2. 이해	3. 확장
• 본책 p.12–17 • 온라인 단어 학습	• 본책 p.18–21 • 별책 p.2–3	• 본책 p.22–24	• 본책 p.26–31 • 온라인 단어 학습	• 본책 p.32–35 • 별책 p.4–5	• 본책 p.36–38
월 일	월 일	월 일	월 일	월 일	월 일
Unit 3			**Unit 4**		
1. 읽기	2. 이해	3. 확장	1. 읽기	2. 이해	3. 확장
• 본책 p.40–45 • 온라인 단어 학습	• 본책 p.46–49 • 별책 p.6–7	• 본책 p.50–52	• 본책 p.54–59 • 온라인 단어 학습	• 본책 p.60–63 • 별책 p.8–9	• 본책 p.64–66
월 일	월 일	월 일	월 일	월 일	월 일
Review Test 1 p.67-70					월 일
Unit 5			**Unit 6**		
1. 읽기	2. 이해	3. 확장	1. 읽기	2. 이해	3. 확장
• 본책 p.72–77 • 온라인 단어 학습	• 본책 p.78–81 • 별책 p.10–11	• 본책 p.82–84	• 본책 p.86–91 • 온라인 단어 학습	• 본책 p.92–95 • 별책 p.12–13	• 본책 p.96–98
월 일	월 일	월 일	월 일	월 일	월 일
Unit 7			**Unit 8**		
1. 읽기	2. 이해	3. 확장	1. 읽기	2. 이해	3. 확장
• 본책 p.100–105 • 온라인 단어 학습	• 본책 p.106–109 • 별책 p.14–15	• 본책 p.110–112	• 본책 p.114–119 • 온라인 단어 학습	• 본책 p.120–123 • 별책 p.16–17	• 본책 p.124–126
월 일	월 일	월 일	월 일	월 일	월 일
Review Test 2 p.127-130					월 일

8주 완성 학습 스케줄

Week	학습	내용	날짜
Week 1 Unit 1	1. 읽기	• 본책 p.12–17 • 온라인 단어 학습	월 일
	2. 이해	• 본책 p.18–21 • 별책 p.2–3	월 일
	3. 확장	• 본책 p.22–24	월 일
Week 2 Unit 2	1. 읽기	• 본책 p.26–31 • 온라인 단어 학습	월 일
	2. 이해	• 본책 p.32–35 • 별책 p.4–5	월 일
	3. 확장	• 본책 p.36–38	월 일
Week 3 Unit 3	1. 읽기	• 본책 p.40–45 • 온라인 단어 학습	월 일
	2. 이해	• 본책 p.46–49 • 별책 p.6–7	월 일
	3. 확장	• 본책 p.50–52	월 일
Week 4 Unit 4	1. 읽기	• 본책 p.54–59 • 온라인 단어 학습	월 일
	2. 이해	• 본책 p.60–63 • 별책 p.8–9	월 일
	3. 확장	• 본책 p.64–66	월 일
	Review Test 1 p.67-70		월 일
Week 5 Unit 5	1. 읽기	• 본책 p.72–77 • 온라인 단어 학습	월 일
	2. 이해	• 본책 p.78–81 • 별책 p.10–11	월 일
	3. 확장	• 본책 p.82–84	월 일
Week 6 Unit 6	1. 읽기	• 본책 p.86–91 • 온라인 단어 학습	월 일
	2. 이해	• 본책 p.92–95 • 별책 p.12–13	월 일
	3. 확장	• 본책 p.96–98	월 일
Week 7 Unit 7	1. 읽기	• 본책 p.100–105 • 온라인 단어 학습	월 일
	2. 이해	• 본책 p.106–109 • 별책 p.14–15	월 일
	3. 확장	• 본책 p.110–112	월 일
Week 8 Unit 8	1. 읽기	• 본책 p.114–119 • 온라인 단어 학습	월 일
	2. 이해	• 본책 p.120–123 • 별책 p.16–17	월 일
	3. 확장	• 본책 p.124–126	월 일
	Review Test 2 p.127-130		월 일

Key Words를 확실하게 익히는 온라인 단어 학습!

온라인 학습으로 지문을 이해하는 데 필요한 단어들을 꼼꼼하게 익혀요. 단어의 철자와 의미를 정확하게 알게 돼요.

길벗스쿨 e클래스에서 오디오 바로 듣기

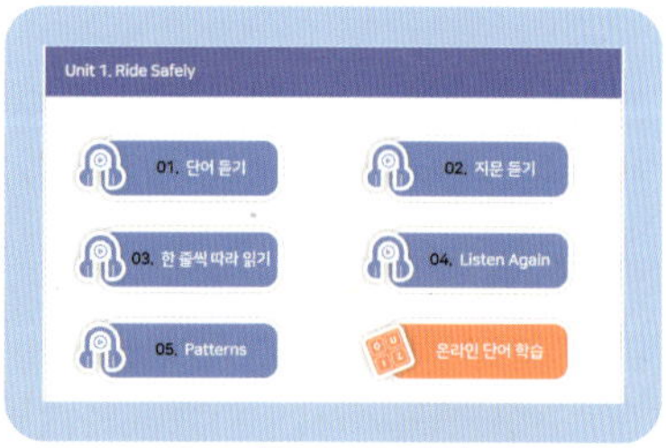

eclass.gilbut.co.kr에서 학습에 필요한 모든 음원을 제공합니다. 오디오 번호를 찾아 한 번만 탭 하면 해당 유닛의 단어와 스토리 음원을 바로 들을 수 있어요.

Practice Book으로 꼼꼼한 보충 학습!

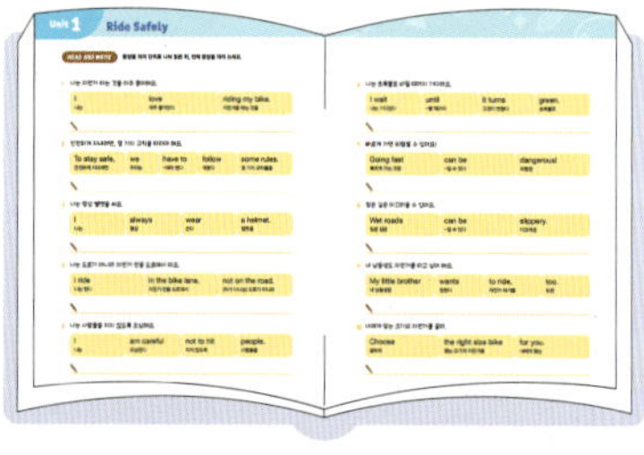

문장을 의미 단위로 나누어 읽고 쓰며 문장 감각을 키우는 별책 연습서를 제공해요.

Unit 1

Ride Safely

STEP 1 읽기 핵심 단어를 익혀서 스토리 듣고 읽기

STEP 2 이해 읽은 내용을 점검하여 스토리 이해하기

STEP 3 확장 필수 문형 학습으로 문장 이해력 키우기

Key Words

- 다음 단어들을 하나씩 손으로 짚으며 잘 들어 보세요. 01

helmet

protect

ride

road

hill

puddle

slippery

size

온라인 단어 학습

온라인 학습으로 단어를 꼼꼼히 익혀요.

A 단어와 우리말 뜻을 알맞게 연결하세요.

1	protect	보호하다
2	hill	크기
3	size	언덕
4	slippery	미끄러운

B 우리말 뜻에 맞는 단어가 되도록 빈칸에 알맞은 글자를 쓰세요.

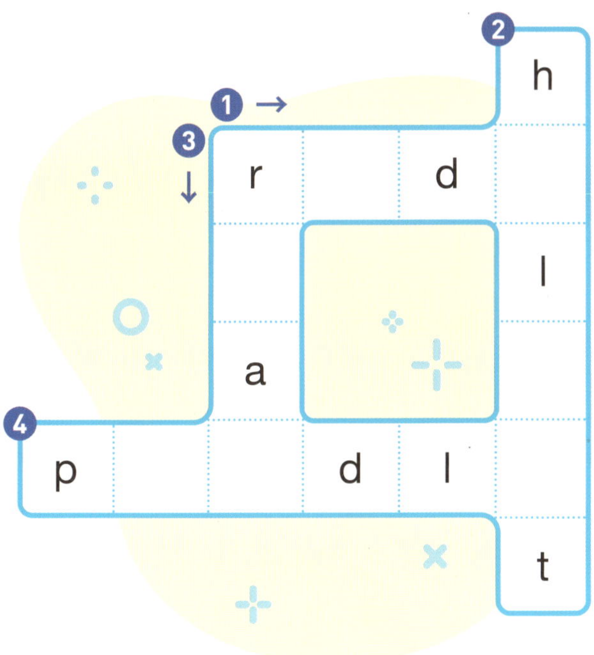

1 (자전거 등을) 타다

2 헬멧

3 도로, 길

4 물웅덩이

Ride Safely

I love riding my bike.

To stay safe, **we have to** follow some rules.

I always wear a helmet.

It protects my head.

stay 상태를 유지하다

I ride in the bike lane, not on the road.

I am careful not to hit people.

I always stop at a red light.

I wait until it turns green.

bike lane 자전거 전용 도로 | careful 조심하는 | hit 치다

I go slow on hills.

Going fast can be dangerous!

Watch out for puddles!

Wet roads can be slippery.

My little brother wants to ride, too.

"One more rule! Choose the right size bike for you."

I help him onto his tricycle.

"Now you have the perfect bike!"

choose 고르다 | tricycle 세발자전거 | perfect 완벽한, ~에 꼭 맞는

Comprehension

A 보기에서 알맞은 단어를 골라 빈칸에 쓰세요.

slippery　lane　ride　helmet　hill

1 

My little brother wants to ________, too.

2 

Wet roads can be ________.

3 

I always wear a ________.

4 

I go slow on ________s.

5 

I ride in the bike ________, not on the road.

B 그림을 보고 알맞은 문장에 ✓ 표시를 하세요.

1 

☐ Watch out for puddles!

☐ Watch out for people!

2 

☐ I help him onto his tricycle.

☐ I ride in the bike lane, not on the road.

3 

☐ I always stop at a red light.

☐ I always stop at a green light.

C 다음 문장이 옳으면 T(True), 틀리면 F(False)에 동그라미 하세요.

1 This story is about how to ride a bike fast. (T) (F)

2 A helmet protects his arms. (T) (F)

3 The boy rides his bike carefully. (T) (F)

D 빈칸에 알맞은 단어를 넣어 자전거 안전 규칙을 완성하세요.

You should ...

- always wear a ______________.
- ______________ at a red light.
- go ______________ on hills.
- watch out for puddles.
- choose the right ______________ bike for you.

slow	stop	helmet	size

Think & Say

신호등이 빨간 불로 바뀌면 어떻게 해야 할까요?

☐ Cross before any cars come. (차들이 오기 전에 건너요.)

☐ Stop and get off my bike. (멈추고 자전거에서 내려요.)

☐ Ring the bell and cross the street. (벨을 울리고 길을 건너요.)

• cross 건너다

Listen Again

● 스토리를 다시 들으며 빈칸에 알맞은 단어를 써 넣으세요. 04

I love riding my ________. To stay safe, we have to follow some rules.

I always wear a ________. It ________s my head.

I ride in the ________, not on the road. I am careful not to hit people.

I always stop at a red light. I wait until it turns green.

I go slow on ________s. Going fast can be dangerous!

Watch out for ________s! Wet roads can be ________.

My little brother wants to ________, too.

"One more rule! Choose the right ________ bike for you."

I help him onto his ________. "Now you have the perfect bike!"

helmet
protect
puddle
bike lane
hill
tricycle
size
bike
slippery
ride

Sentence Patterns

● 다음 필수 문형을 다양한 예문에 적용해 보세요. 05

1 We have to ________ . 우리는 ~해야 해요.

① 우리는 몇 가지 규칙들을 따라야 해요.

We have to follow some rules .

② 우리는 우리의 친구를 도와야 해요.

We have to ________ .

③ 우리는 플라스틱을 재활용해야 해요.

We have to ________ .

2 I wait until ________ . 나는 ~할 때까지 기다려요.

① 나는 초록불로 바뀔 때까지 기다려요.

I wait until it turns green .

② 나는 비가 멈출 때까지 기다려요.

I wait until ________ .

③ 나는 페인트가 마를 때까지 기다려요.

I wait until ________ .

Word Box

- recycle plastic 플라스틱을 재활용하다
- help our friends 우리의 친구를 돕다
- the paint dries 페인트가 마르다
- the rain stops 비가 멈추다
- bees 벌들
- rocks 바위들

3 Watch out for ______ ! ~을 조심해!

① 물웅덩이를 조심해!

Watch out for puddles !

② 바위들을 조심해!

Watch out for ______ !

③ 벌들을 조심해!

Watch out for ______ !

Try Writing

배운 필수 문형을 활용해 영작해 보세요.

1 

깨진 유리를 조심해! (the broken glass)

______

2 

우리는 손을 씻어야 해요. (wash our hands)

______

3 

나는 물이 끓을 때까지 기다려요. (the water boils)

______

Think More

Ride Safely!

★ 알맞은 단어를 골라 자전거를 안전하게 타는 방법을 완성하세요.

Wear a (helmet / hat).

Wear (dark / bright) clothes.

Use the (road / bike lane).

Stop at a (green / red) light.

Look (one / both) ways before crossing.

Don't go too (fast / slow) on hills.

• dark 어두운 bright 밝은

Plus 자전거 도로는 자전거가 다닐 수 있도록 따로 마련된 길이에요. 자전거는 자동차보다 작고 느려서 차도에서 달리면 위험해요. 또 인도에서는 걷는 사람과도 부딪힐 수 있어요. 그래서 차도와 인도, 자전거 도로로 구분하면, 서로 방해받지 않고 모두가 더 편리하고 안전하게 이동할 수 있습니다.

Unit 2

My Summer Vacation

STEP 1 읽기 핵심 단어를 익혀서 스토리 듣고 읽기

STEP 2 이해 읽은 내용을 점검하여 스토리 이해하기

STEP 3 확장 필수 문형 학습으로 문장 이해력 키우기

Key Words

● 다음 단어들을 하나씩 손으로 짚으며 잘 들어 보세요. 06

vacation

late

schedule

write

wake up

woke up 일어났다

bored

laugh

jump rope

온라인 단어 학습

온라인 학습으로 단어를 꼼꼼히 익혀요.

A 단어와 우리말 뜻을 알맞게 연결하세요.

1 wake up	• •	방학
2 jump rope	• •	줄넘기를 하다
3 schedule	• •	(잠에서) 깨다, 일어나다
4 vacation	• •	일정, 스케줄

B 다음 우리말 뜻에 맞는 단어를 찾아 동그라미 하고 한 번 쓰세요.

b	i	u	r	e	z	o	w
y	s	d	m	j	x	c	r
k	b	o	r	e	d	a	i
t	j	q	o	i	o	y	t
n	f	l	e	b	v	q	e
w	j	a	t	r	c	m	h
c	k	t	l	a	u	g	h
g	u	e	i	n	d	s	f

1 늦게

l

2 웃다

l

3 지루해하는

b

4 쓰다, 적다

w

My Summer Vacation

Summer vacation began today.

I was lazy, and I got up late.

I played with my friends all day.

"**How about** making a daily schedule?" Mom says.

begin 시작되다, 시작하다 (과거형 began) | lazy 게으른 |
get up 일어나다 (과거형 got up) | all day 하루 종일 | daily 매일의

I sit and write my daily schedule.

"Wake up at 7. Eat lunch at 12. Read at 2."

Mom says, "It's a great plan!"

But **it looks** boring **to me.**

plan 계획 | boring 지루한

The next day, **I tried to** follow my schedule.

I woke up at 7,

but I fell asleep again.

I opened a book at 2,

but I got bored.

I started playing computer games for fun.

fall asleep 잠들다 (과거형 fell asleep) | get bored 지루해지다 (과거형 got bored)

"Oh no, today didn't go as planned."

Mom laughs.

"You can still jump rope before bed!"

"Yay! I did one thing on my schedule today!"

before ~전에

Comprehension

A 보기에서 알맞은 단어를 골라 빈칸에 쓰세요.

wake up	jump rope	vacation	schedule	bored

1 

I opened a book at 2, but I got ________.

2 

"You can still ________ before bed!"

3 

Summer ________ began today.

4 

"________ at 7. Eat lunch at 12. Read at 2."

5 

"How about making a daily ________?"

B 그림을 보고 알맞은 문장에 ✓ 표시를 하세요.

1

- [ ] I was lazy, and I got up late.
- [ ] I was lazy, and I opened a book.

2

- [ ] I played with my friends all day.
- [ ] I jumped rope all day.

3

- [ ] I started reading a book for fun.
- [ ] I started playing computer games for fun.

C 다음 문장이 옳으면 T(True), 틀리면 F(False)에 동그라미 하세요.

1. The boy jumped rope before bed. (T) (F)
2. The boy said, "It's a great plan!" (T) (F)
3. The boy woke up late on the first day. (T) (F)

D 계획표를 보고, 계획한 일과 실제로 한 일을 구분하여 기호를 쓰세요.

My Daily Schedule (계획)	What I Really Did (내가 실제로 한 일)
Wake up at 7.	
	I opened a book, but I got bored.
Jump rope at 7.	

ⓐ I did it!

ⓑ Read at 2.

ⓒ I woke up at 7, but I fell asleep again.

Think & Say

이 글에서 배울 점을 골라 ✓ 표시하세요.

- ☐ Jump rope is good for your health. (줄넘기는 건강에 좋아요.)
- ☐ It's good to make a plan. (계획을 세우는 것이 좋아요.)
- ☐ You should read books every day. (매일 책을 읽어야 해요.)

Listen Again

스토리를 다시 들으며 빈칸에 알맞은 단어를 써 넣으세요. 09

Summer ________ began today. I was lazy, and I got up ________.

I played with my friends all day. "How about making a daily ________?" Mom says.

I sit and ________ my daily schedule. "________ at 7. Eat lunch at 12. Read at 2." Mom says, "It's a great plan!" But it looks boring to me.

The next day, I tried to ________ my schedule. I woke up at 7, but I fell asleep again. I ________ed a book at 2, but I got ________. I started playing computer games for fun.

"Oh no, today didn't go as planned." Mom ________s. "You can still jump ________ before bed!"

"Yay! I did one thing on my schedule today!"

write
schedule
open
follow
late
bored
laugh
rope
vacation
wake up

Sentence Patterns

● 다음 필수 문형을 다양한 예문에 적용해 보세요. 10

1 How about ______-ing ? ~하는 게 어때?

❶ 일과표를 만드는 게 어때?

How about making a daily schedule ?

❷ 나무를 심는 게 어때?

How about ______ ?

❸ 영화 보는 게 어때?

How about ______ ?

2 It looks ______ to me. 그것은 나에게 ~해 보여요.

❶ 그것은 나에게 지루해 보여요.

It looks boring to me.

❷ 그것은 나에게 재미있어 보여요.

It looks ______ to me.

❸ 그것은 나에게 무서워 보여요.

It looks ______ to me.

Word Box

- finish my homework 내 숙제를 끝내다
- catch the butterfly 그 나비를 잡다
- watch a movie 영화를 보다
- plant a tree 나무를 심다
- fun 재미있는
- scary 무서운

3 I tried to ______ . 나는 ~하려고 노력했어요.

❶ 나는 내 일정을 따르려고 노력했어요.

I tried to follow my schedule .

❷ 나는 그 나비를 잡으려고 노력했어요.

I tried to ______ .

❸ 나는 내 숙제를 끝내려고 노력했어요.

I tried to ______ .

Try Writing

배운 필수 문형을 활용해 영작해 보세요.

1

책을 읽는 게 어때? (read a book)

______

2

그것은 나에게 흥미로워 보여요. (interesting)

______

3

나는 퍼즐을 풀려고 노력했어요. (solve the puzzle)

______

Think More

My Daily Schedule

★ 나의 방학 생활 계획표를 보고 엄마의 질문에 답하세요.

1. What time do you get up?	I get up at ______ a.m.
2. When do you read books?	I read books at ______ p.m.
3. What do you do from 9 to 11a.m.?	I ______________________.
4. What do you do after dinner?	I ____________ after dinner.

Plus 방학을 계획 없이 보내면 금방 지나가 버려요. 그래서 계획을 세우는 것이 중요합니다. 먼저, 방학 동안 꼭 이루고 싶은 목표를 정하고 그 목표를 매일 실천할 수 있는 작은 분량으로 나누어 보세요. 그리고 계획을 지킨 날을 표시해 보세요. 성취감이 쌓일수록 꾸준히 지킬 수 있고 보람도 더 크게 느낄 수 있어요.

Unit 3

The Rainy Barbecue

STEP 1 읽기 핵심 단어를 익혀서 스토리 듣고 읽기

STEP 2 이해 읽은 내용을 점검하여 스토리 이해하기

STEP 3 확장 필수 문형 학습으로 문장 이해력 키우기

Key Words

- 다음 단어들을 하나씩 손으로 짚으며 잘 들어 보세요. 11

set up

light

lit 불을 붙였다

dark

yesterday

forecast

pour

sandwich

picnic

온라인 단어 학습

온라인 학습으로 단어를 꼼꼼히 익혀요.

A 단어와 우리말 뜻을 알맞게 연결하세요.

1 sandwich	소풍
2 yesterday	어제
3 picnic	샌드위치
4 set up	준비하다

B 다음 우리말 뜻에 맞는 단어를 찾아 동그라미 하고 한 번 쓰세요.

f	o	r	e	c	a	s	t
t	w	h	r	o	p	m	a
s	d	e	t	f	i	c	l
b	a	g	k	j	l	w	e
q	r	p	o	u	r	n	y
i	k	z	m	y	g	s	l
v	j	c	q	a	t	h	d
l	i	g	h	t	w	e	o

1 검은, 어두운

d

2 불을 붙이다

l

3 예보

f

4 (비가) 마구 쏟아지다

p

1 전체 지문 듣기 12 2 한 줄씩 따라 읽기 13 3 스스로 읽기

The Rainy Barbecue

Alex's family is having a barbecue today.

"**It'll be** sunny **all day,**" Dad said.

They set up the grill.

Dad lit the fire for the barbecue.

barbecue 바비큐 파티

Suddenly, a strong wind blew.

The fire **went out**, and Mom's scarf flew away!

"My scarf!" Mom ran after it.

"It's not really sunny today!"

suddenly 갑자기 | **blow** (바람이) 불다 (과거형 **blew**) | **scarf** 스카프 |
fly away 날아가다 (과거형 **flew away**) | **run after** ~을 따라가다 (과거형 **ran after**)

Dark clouds appeared in the sky.
Soon, it started to rain.
"It's not sunny at all," Alex said.
Everyone ran for cover.

Dad checked his phone.
"Oh no! I looked at yesterday's forecast!"

appear 나타나다 | look at ~을 보다

It poured, and the wind grew stronger.

The tent blew away.

Mom took out our sandwiches.

"**It's fun to** have a picnic in the rain," Mom said.

grow 커지다 (과거형 grew) | blow away (바람에) 날아가다 (과거형 blew away) |
take out 꺼내다 (과거형 took out)

Comprehension

A 보기에서 알맞은 단어를 골라 빈칸에 쓰세요.

dark	forecast	set up	sandwich	pour

1 

It ______ed, and the wind grew stronger.

2 

______ clouds appeared in the sky.

3 

They ______ the grill.

4 

Mom took out our ______es.

5 

“Oh no! I looked at yesterday’s ______!”

B 그림을 보고 알맞은 문장에 ✓ 표시를 하세요.

1

- [ ] Dad lit the fire for the barbecue.
- [ ] Dad checked his phone.

2

- [ ] It'll be sunny all day.
- [ ] It's not sunny at all.

3

- [ ] They ran for cover.
- [ ] They took out their sandwiches.

C 다음 문장이 옳으면 T(True), 틀리면 F(False)에 동그라미 하세요.

1 Dad said it would be sunny all day. T F

2 A strong wind blew Mom's hat away. T F

3 Dad checked yesterday's forecast by mistake. T F

• by mistake 실수로

D 이야기 순서에 맞게 빈칸에 알맞은 기호를 쓰세요.

ⓐ Mom's scarf flew away!

ⓑ Dark clouds appeared, and it started to rain.

ⓒ Mom said, "It's fun to have a picnic in the rain."

ⓓ Dad said, "It'll be sunny all day!"

☐ → ☐ → ☐ → ☐

Think & Say

가족과 캠핑할 때, 내가 가장 좋아하는 일은 무엇인가요?

- ☐ grill the food
- ☐ play games
- ☐ go fishing
- ☐ eat together

I like to ______________ when I go camping with my family.

Listen Again

● 스토리를 다시 들으며 빈칸에 알맞은 단어를 써 넣으세요. 14

Alex's family is having a ______ today. "It'll be sunny all day," Dad said.
They ______ the grill. Dad ______ the fire for the barbecue.

Suddenly, a strong ______ blew. The fire went out, and Mom's scarf flew away! "My scarf!" Mom ran after it. "It's not really ______ today!"

Dark clouds ______ ed in the sky. Soon, it started to rain. "It's not sunny at all," Alex said. Everyone ran for cover.
Dad checked his phone. "Oh no! I looked at yesterday's ______!"

It ______ ed, and the wind grew stronger. The tent blew away. Mom took out our ______ es. "It's fun to have a ______ in the rain," Mom said.

pour
lit
sandwich
picnic
barbecue
sunny
appear
set up
forecast
wind

Sentence Patterns

● 다음 필수 문형을 다양한 예문에 적용해 보세요. 15

1 It'll be ______ all day. 하루 종일 (날씨가) ~할 거예요.

① 하루 종일 화창할 거예요.

It'll be sunny all day.

② 하루 종일 비가 올 거예요.

It'll be ______ all day.

③ 하루 종일 눈이 올 거예요.

It'll be ______ all day.

2 ______ went out. ~가 꺼졌어요.

① 불이 꺼졌어요.

The fire went out.

② 전등이 꺼졌어요.

______ went out.

③ 촛불이 꺼졌어요.

______ went out.

Word Box

- open a gift 선물을 열다
- kick a ball 공을 차다
- snowy 눈이 내리는
- rainy 비가 내리는
- the light 전등
- the candle 촛불

3 It's fun to ______ . ~하는 것은 재미있어요.

① 소풍 가는 것은 재미있어요.

It's fun to have a picnic .

② 공을 차는 것은 재미있어요.

It's fun to ______ .

③ 선물을 여는 것은 재미있어요.

It's fun to ______ .

Try Writing

배운 필수 문형을 활용해 영작해 보세요.

1

하루 종일 바람이 불 거예요. (windy)

______

2

손전등이 꺼졌어요. (the flashlight)

______

3

사진을 찍는 것은 재미있어요. (take pictures)

______

Think More

The Weather Forecast

★ 다음 주 일기 예보를 보고 대화를 완성하세요.

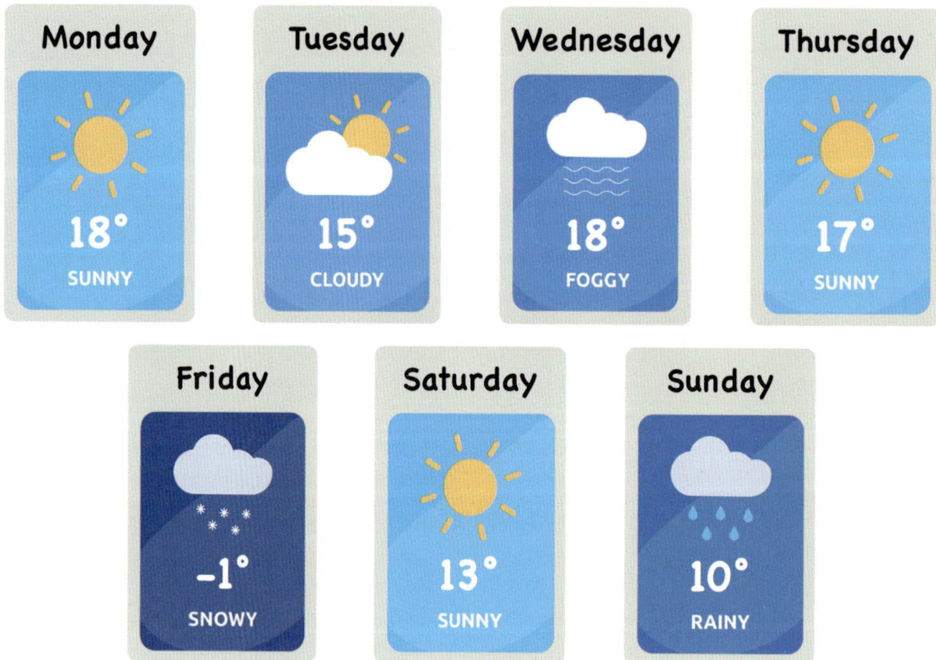

How many days will be sunny?

There will be ________ sunny days.

Which day will be cloudy?

It will be cloudy on ________________.

Which day will be rainy?

It will be rainy on ________________.

Which day will be the coldest?

The coldest day will be ________________.

• coldest 가장 추운

Plus 날씨는 기상청의 과학자들이 여러 가지 도구를 사용해 예보해요. 위성, 레이더, 슈퍼컴퓨터로 구름의 움직임과 바람의 세기를 계산해요. 이렇게 모은 자료를 바탕으로 내일 비가 올지, 해가 뜰지를 예측하고 우리는 그 정보를 보고 우산을 챙기거나 나들이 준비를 할 수 있어요.

Unit 4

The Flying Helpers

STEP 1 읽기 핵심 단어를 익혀서 스토리 듣고 읽기

STEP 2 이해 읽은 내용을 점검하여 스토리 이해하기

STEP 3 확장 필수 문형 학습으로 문장 이해력 키우기

Key Words

- 다음 단어들을 하나씩 손으로 짚으며 잘 들어 보세요. 16

drone

farmer

field

check

crop

crack

wild

traffic

온라인 단어 학습

온라인 학습으로 단어를 꼼꼼히 익혀요.

A 단어와 우리말 뜻을 알맞게 연결하세요.

1	traffic	야생의
2	crop	농작물
3	wild	점검하다, 살피다
4	check	차량들, 교통

B 우리말 뜻에 맞는 단어가 되도록 빈칸에 알맞은 글자를 쓰세요.

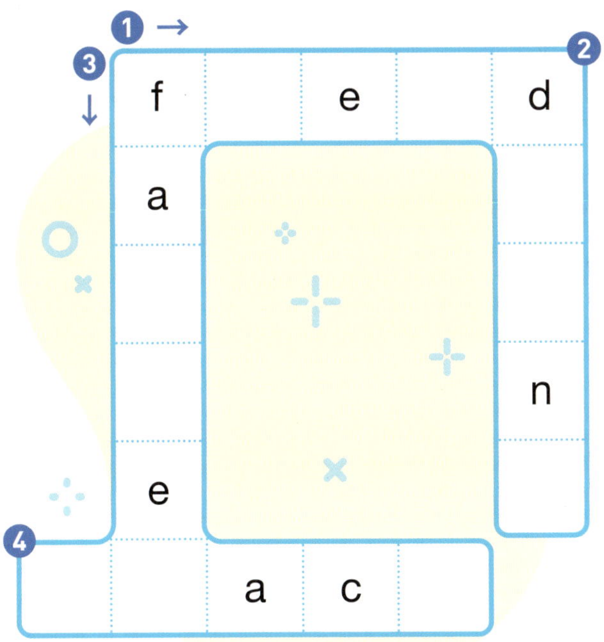

1 들판, 밭

2 드론

3 농부

4 (갈라져 생긴) 금

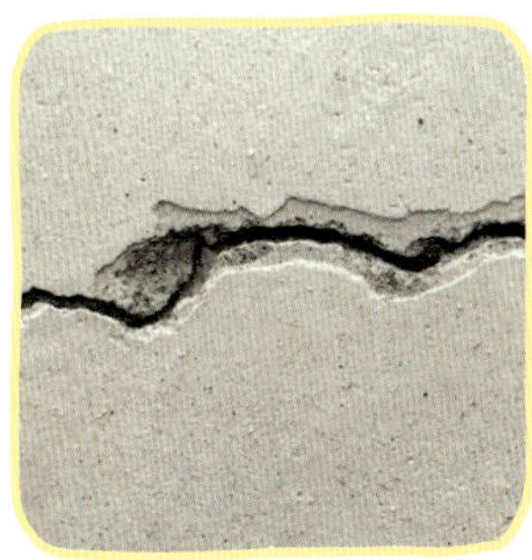

The Flying Helpers

Ring! Ring! The Drone Center gets many calls.

People need flying helpers.

Drones are ready to help!

many 많은 | flying 날아다니는

A drone can help farmers.

It flies over a field.

It checks if the crops are healthy.

A drone can help firefighters.

It can find people in danger.

over ~위를 | **in danger** 위험에 처한

A drone can help engineers.

It checks tall buildings.

It looks for cracks or other problems.

A drone can help scientists.

It watches wild animals without scaring them.

engineer 기술자 | look for 찾다 | scientist 과학자 | scare 겁주다

Maybe we will have drone taxis in the near future.

You could fly above the roads.

No more traffic jams!

Thank you so much, Drone Center!

maybe 어쩌면 | future 미래 | above (~보다) 위에 | traffic jam 교통 체증

Comprehension

A 보기에서 알맞은 단어를 골라 빈칸에 쓰세요.

firefighter   animal   field   crack   taxi

1

A drone can help ______s.

2

A drone looks for ______s or other problems.

3

A drone flies over a ______ .

4

Maybe we will have drone ______s in the near future.

5

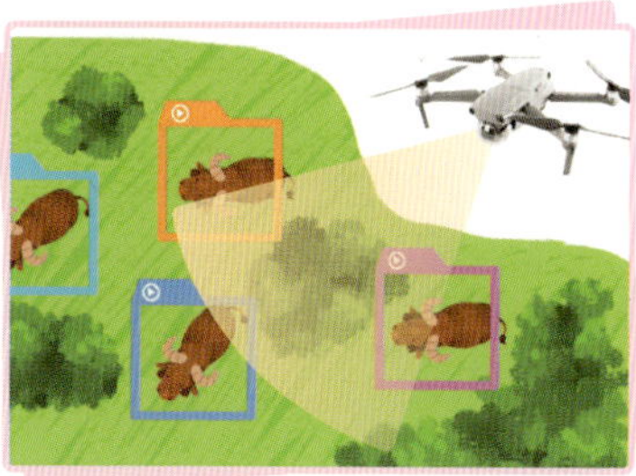

A drone watches wild ______s without scaring them.

B 그림을 보고 알맞은 문장에 ✓ 표시를 하세요.

1 

- [ ] A drone can watch wild animals.
- [ ] A drone can find people in danger.

2 

- [ ] A drone can help farmers.
- [ ] A drone can help engineers.

3 

- [ ] It checks if the crops are healthy.
- [ ] It looks for cracks or other problems.

C 다음 문장이 옳으면 T(True), 틀리면 F(False)에 동그라미 하세요.

1 This story is about how drones help people. T F

2 A drone scares animals in the wild. T F

3 A drone cannot check tall buildings. T F

D 드론이 하는 일을 읽고, 누가 도움을 받는지 ✓ 표시를 하세요.

	farmer	firefighter	engineer	scientist
A drone looks for cracks in tall buildings.				
A drone watches wild animals.				
A drone checks if the crops are healthy.				
A drone finds people in danger.				

Think & Say

드론이 나를 도와준다면, 무엇을 해주면 좋을까요?

- ☐ carry my school bag
- ☐ walk my dog
- ☐ take cool photos
- ☐ find my lost ball

• lost 잃어버린

I want a drone to

________________.

Listen Again

● 스토리를 다시 들으며 빈칸에 알맞은 단어를 써 넣으세요. 19

Ring! Ring! The Drone Center gets many calls. People need flying helpers. ________s are ready to help!

A drone can help ________s. It flies over a ________. It checks if the ________s are healthy.

A drone can help ________s. It can find people in danger.

A drone can help engineers. It ________s tall buildings. It looks for ________s or other problems.

A drone can help ________s. It watches wild animals without scaring them.

Maybe we will have drone taxis in the near future. You could ________ above the roads. No more ________ jams! Thank you so much, Drone Center!

check
crack
fly
crop
traffic
drone
firefighter
farmer
field
scientist

Sentence Patterns

● 다음 필수 문형을 다양한 예문에 적용해 보세요. 20

1 It can help ______ . 그것은 ~을 도울 수 있어요.

① 그것은 농부들을 도울 수 있어요.

It can help farmers .

② 그것은 간호사들을 도울 수 있어요.

It can help ______ .

③ 그것은 경찰관들을 도울 수 있어요.

It can help ______ .

2 It checks if ______ . 그것은 ~인지 아닌지를 점검해요.

① 그것은 농작물이 건강한지 아닌지를 점검해요.

It checks if the crops are healthy .

② 그것은 물이 깨끗한지 아닌지를 점검해요.

It checks if ______ .

③ 그것은 동물들이 아픈지 아닌지를 점검해요.

It checks if ______ .

Word Box

- police officers 경찰관들
- the water is clean 물이 깨끗하다
- robot cats 로봇 고양이
- AI doctors 인공지능 의사
- animals are sick 동물들이 아프다
- nurses 간호사들

3 Maybe we will have ______ . 아마도 우리는 ~을 가지게 될 거예요.

❶ 아마도 우리는 드론 택시를 가지게 될 거예요.

Maybe we will have drone taxis .

❷ 아마도 우리는 로봇 고양이를 가지게 될 거예요.

Maybe we will have ______ .

❸ 아마도 우리는 인공지능 의사를 가지게 될 거예요.

Maybe we will have ______ .

Try Writing

배운 필수 문형을 활용해 영작해 보세요.

1

아마도 우리는 하늘을 나는 자동차를 가지게 될 거예요. (flying cars)

______

2

그것은 조종사들을 도울 수 있어요. (pilots)

______

3

그것은 도로가 안전한지 아닌지를 점검해요. (the roads are safe)

______

Think More

What Can Drones Do?

★ 드론이 어떤 일을 할 수 있는지 확인하고, 문장을 완성하세요.

Drones can ______________ small things.

Drones can ______________ plants.

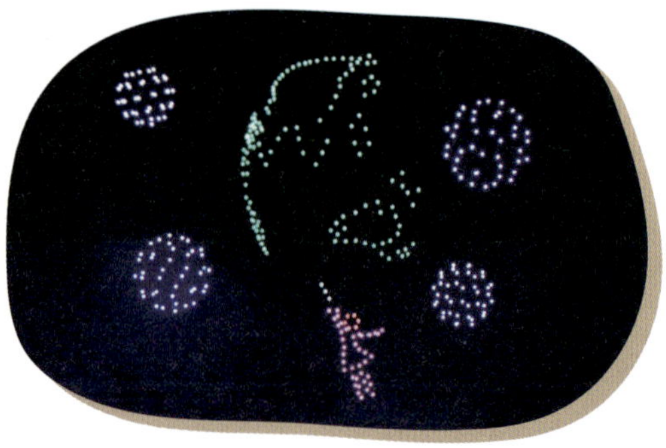

Drones can ______________ beautiful fireworks.

Drones can ______________ lost people.

make	water
find	carry

Drones can film movies.

• fireworks 불꽃놀이 film 촬영하다

Plus 드론이 할 수 있는 일은 정말 놀랍습니다. 불이 난 건물은 연기로 가득 차 앞을 보기가 어렵지만 드론은 사람들이 어디에 있는지 빠르게 알 수 있어요. 넓은 산이나 깊은 바다에서도 드론은 열을 감지해 사람의 체온을 찾아낼 수 있어요. 좁은 골목이나 산간 마을에 약을 실어 나르기도 해요.

Review Test 1
(Unit ① – Unit ④)

/ 25개

A 그림에 알맞은 단어를 고르세요.

1 

ⓐ late ⓑ bored ⓒ careful

2 

ⓐ protect ⓑ ride ⓒ laugh

3 

ⓐ slippery ⓑ wild ⓒ dark

4 

ⓐ field ⓑ traffic ⓒ hill

5 

ⓐ set up ⓑ write ⓒ wake up

6 

ⓐ puddle ⓑ crack ⓒ sandwich

B 그림을 보고 알맞은 문장을 고르세요.

1 

ⓐ I played with my friends all day.

ⓑ I started playing computer games for fun.

2 

ⓐ Going fast on hills can be dangerous!

ⓑ Wet roads can be slippery!

3 

ⓐ It'll be sunny all day.

ⓑ It's not sunny at all.

4 

ⓐ The drone flies over a field.

ⓑ The drone checks tall buildings.

★★

C 알맞은 단어를 골라 문장을 완성하세요.

1 Alex's family ⓐ is ⓑ are having a barbecue today.

2 I love ⓐ ride ⓑ riding my bike.

3 The Drone Center gets many ⓐ call ⓑ calls .

4 I was lazy, and I ⓐ get ⓑ got up late this morning.

D 짧은 글을 읽고 질문에 알맞은 대답을 고르세요.

1 다음 글에 해당하는 날씨 그림을 고르세요.

Dark clouds appeared in the sky.
Soon, it started to rain.
"It's not sunny at all," Alex said.

ⓐ

ⓑ

2 다음 글에서 them이 가리키는 사람은 누구인가요?

A drone can help <u>them</u>.
It checks tall buildings.
It looks for cracks or other problems.

ⓐ engineers

ⓑ firefighters

3 빈칸에 들어갈 알맞은 문장을 고르세요.

To stay safe, we follow some rules.
______________________.
It protects my head.

ⓐ I always wear a helmet.

ⓑ I always stop at a red light.

4 빈칸에 들어갈 알맞은 단어를 고르세요.

I was lazy, and I got up late.
"How about making a daily
__________?" Mom says.

ⓐ party

ⓑ schedule

E 필수 패턴을 활용해 우리말에 알맞은 영어 문장을 완성하세요.

How about ______?
It's fun to ______.
It can help ______.
Watch out for ______!

1 나무를 심는 게 어때?

→ ______________________ planting a tree?

2 공을 차는 것은 재미있어요.

→ ______________________ kick a ball.

3 바위들을 조심해!

→ ______________________ rocks!

4 그것은 경찰관들을 도울 수 있어요.

→ ______________________ police officers.

F 우리말에 알맞은 영어 문장을 쓰세요.

1 하루 종일 눈이 올 거예요. (be, snowy, it'll, all day)

→ ______________________________________.

2 나는 내 숙제를 끝내려고 노력했어요. (tried to, my homework, I, finish)

→ ______________________________________.

3 우리는 플라스틱을 재활용해야 해요. (plastic, recycle, we, have to)

→ ______________________________________.

Unit 5

Pick a Movie!

STEP 1 읽기 핵심 단어를 익혀서 스토리 듣고 읽기

STEP 2 이해 읽은 내용을 점검하여 스토리 이해하기

STEP 3 확장 필수 문형 학습으로 문장 이해력 키우기

Key Words

- 다음 단어들을 하나씩 손으로 짚으며 잘 들어 보세요. 21

movie

superhero

brave

fight

finger

wizard

choose

decide

온라인 단어 학습

온라인 학습으로 단어를 꼼꼼히 익혀요.

A 단어와 우리말 뜻을 알맞게 연결하세요.

1	choose	• •	손가락
2	wizard	• •	슈퍼히어로
3	superhero	• •	마법사
4	finger	• •	선택하다, 고르다

B 다음 우리말 뜻에 맞는 단어를 찾아 동그라미 하고 한 번 쓰세요.

h	y	d	t	m	a	d	i
o	j	s	g	p	r	e	v
b	r	a	v	e	u	c	k
r	f	n	w	q	l	i	z
c	i	p	a	b	t	d	d
y	g	u	h	j	g	e	s
l	h	t	m	o	v	i	e
u	t	e	k	b	x	n	f

1 용감한
b

2 영화
m

3 싸우다
f

4 결정하다
d

Pick a Movie!

Emma and her friends go to the movies.

They look at the movie posters.

"So many choices!" Emma says.

They talk about which movie to see.

pick 고르다, 선택 | go to the movies 영화를 보러 가다 | choice 선택 | which 어느, 어떤

Jack wants to see the superhero movie.
"Superheroes are brave and strong.
They fight bad guys and help people."

He holds out his hand
like a superhero.

bad guy 악당 | hold out 내밀다

The fantasy movie is Sophia's pick.

"**There are** flying books and talking hats.

The story will be full of surprises!"

Sophia waves her finger

like a wizard.

fantasy 공상, 환상 | full 가득한 | surprise 놀라움

Emma chooses the animal movie.

"The animals go on a trip together.

It looks exciting," she says.

"**It's hard to** decide.

Let's get some popcorn first!" Jack says.

exciting 신나는 | hard 어려운, 힘든

Comprehension

A 보기에서 알맞은 단어를 골라 빈칸에 쓰세요.

movie   decide   fight   superhero   animal

1 

"It's hard to ________ . Let's get some popcorn first!"

2 

Emma chooses the ________ movie.

3 

He holds out his hand like a ________ .

4 

"They ________ bad guys and help people."

5 

They talk about which ________ to see.

B 그림을 보고 알맞은 문장에 ✓ 표시를 하세요.

1

☐ Sophia fights bad guys.

☐ Sophia waves her finger like a wizard.

2

☐ They look at the books.

☐ They look at the movie posters.

3

☐ The animals go on a trip together.

☐ The animals help people.

C 다음 문장이 옳으면 T(True), 틀리면 F(False)에 동그라미 하세요.

1. Emma and her friends go on a trip. T F
2. They talk about which game to play. T F
3. There are talking hats in the superhero movie. T F

D 빈칸에 알맞은 단어를 써서 영화 소개를 완성하세요.

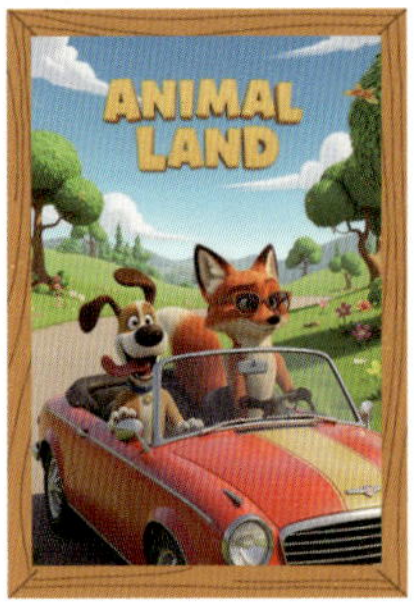

the animal movie
- animals going on a ________
- an ________ story

the superhero movie
- brave and ________ superheroes
- fighting bad guys and helping people

the fantasy movie
- ________ books and talking hats
- a story full of ________s

strong	flying	surprise	trip	exciting

Think & Say

아주 재미있게 본 영화는 어떤 종류의 영화인가요?

- ☐ a comedy movie
- ☐ a fantasy movie
- ☐ an action movie
- ☐ an animated movie

I like ________(종류).
My favorite movie is ________(제목).

Listen Again

● 스토리를 다시 들으며 빈칸에 알맞은 단어를 써 넣으세요. (24)

Emma and her friends go to the movies. They look at the movie ________s. "So many choices!" Emma says. They talk about which ________ to see.

Jack wants to see the superhero movie. "Superheroes are ________ and strong. They fight bad guys and help people."
He holds out his hand like a ________.

The ________ movie is Sophia's pick. "There are flying books and talking hats. The story will be full of ________s!"
Sophia waves her finger like a ________.

Emma ________s the animal movie.
"The animals go on a ________ together.
It looks exciting," she says.
"It's hard to ________. Let's get some popcorn first!" Jack says.

wizard
brave
choose
poster
trip
surprise
superhero
decide
movie
fantasy

Sentence Patterns

● 다음 필수 문형을 다양한 예문에 적용해 보세요. 25

1 They talk about ______ . 그들은 ~에 대해 이야기해요.

① 그들은 어떤 영화를 볼지에 대해 이야기해요.

They talk about which movie to see.

② 그들은 어떤 게임을 할지에 대해 이야기해요.

They talk about ______________.

③ 그들은 어느 버스를 탈지에 대해 이야기해요.

They talk about ______________.

2 There are ______ . ~들이 있어요.

① 하늘을 나는 책들이 있어요.

There are flying books.

② 말하는 앵무새들이 있어요.

There are ______________.

③ 노래하는 고양이들이 있어요.

There are ______________.

Word Box

- which game to play 어떤 게임을 할지
- which bus to take 어느 버스를 탈지
- talking parrots 말하는 앵무새들
- singing cats 노래하는 고양이들
- remember 기억하다
- wait 기다리다

3 It's hard to ______ . ~하기 어려워요.

❶ 결정하기 어려워요.

It's hard to decide .

❷ 기다리기 어려워요.

It's hard to ______ .

❸ 기억하기 어려워요.

It's hard to ______ .

Try Writing

배운 필수 문형을 활용해 영작해 보세요.

1 

펄럭이는 깃발들이 있어요. (waving flags)

______

2 

그들은 어느 셔츠를 입을지에 대해 이야기해요. (which shirt to wear)

______

3 

웃기 어려워요. (smile)

______

Think More

At the Movies

★ 아이들이 보고 싶어 하는 영화는 무엇일까요? 잘 읽고 영화 제목을 쓰세요.

NOW SHOWING

Space Journey	9:00
Superhero Power	9:30
Animal Friends	10:00
A Day in the Park	10:30
The Wizard's Dragon	11:00

It's a movie with a brave and strong superhero. It will be exciting.
It starts at 9:30.

I choose the fantasy movie. A dragon and a wizard will have an adventure.
It starts at 11:00.

• journey 여행

Plus 영화에는 다양한 종류가 있어요. 신비로운 판타지 영화(fantasy movie), 웃긴 코미디 영화(comedy), 신나는 액션 영화(action movie)처럼요. 종류마다 주는 재미와 감정은 다르지만, 모두 우리의 마음을 움직이고 상상력을 키워줍니다. 그래서 영화를 보는 일은 단순한 즐거움을 넘어 특별한 경험이 되지요.

Unit 6

The Lost Kitten

STEP 1 읽기 핵심 단어를 익혀서 스토리 듣고 읽기

STEP 2 이해 읽은 내용을 점검하여 스토리 이해하기

STEP 3 확장 필수 문형 학습으로 문장 이해력 키우기

Key Words

● 다음 단어들을 하나씩 손으로 짚으며 잘 들어 보세요. 26

find

found 찾았다

kitten

hide

hiding 숨어 있는

gray

lost

string

poster

call

온라인 단어 학습

온라인 학습으로 단어를 꼼꼼히 익혀요.

A 단어와 우리말 뜻을 알맞게 연결하세요.

1	string	잃어버린, 길을 잃은
2	call	새끼 고양이
3	kitten	전화하다
4	lost	끈

B 우리말 뜻에 맞는 단어가 되도록 빈칸에 알맞은 글자를 쓰세요.

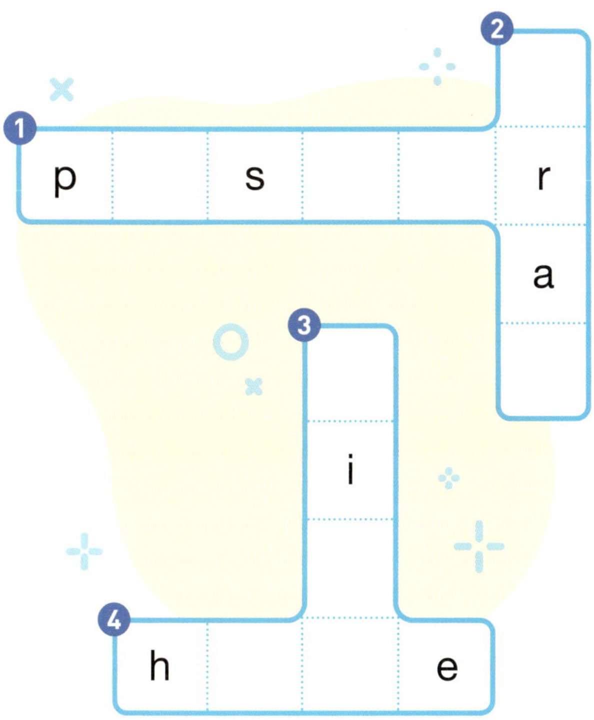

1 포스터, 벽보

2 회색의, 회색

3 (우연히) 찾다, 발견하다

4 숨다

The Lost Kitten

April 1

Today, **I found** a kitten **in** my backyard.

It was hiding in a bush.

It was small and gray.

Mom said, "Let's help the lost kitten."

backyard 뒷마당 | bush 덤불

April 3

I named the kitten Milo.

Milo likes to play with string.

We made a poster: "Is This Your Cat?"

We put it up at the park.

name 이름을 지어주다 | make 만들다 (과거형 made) |
put up 내붙이다, 게시하다 | friendly 상냥한

April 7

A lady called about Milo.

She said, "That's my kitten!"

She came and took Milo home.

I was sad to say good-bye but happy Milo found his family.

come 오다 (과거형 came) | take 데리고 가다 (과거형 took)

April 10

I visited Milo at his house.

He sat on my lap and purred.

The lady said, "Thank you for saving him."

"I'm so glad he is back home," I smiled.

sit 앉다 (과거형 sat) | lap 무릎 | purr 가르랑거리다 | save 구하다 | glad 기쁜

Comprehension

A 보기에서 알맞은 단어를 골라 빈칸에 쓰세요.

gray family poster visit string

1 

We made a ______ :
"Is This Your Cat?"

2 

It was small and ______ .

3 

I ______ ed Milo at his house.

4 

Milo likes to play with ______ .

5 

I was sad to say good-bye but happy
Milo found his ______ .

B 그림을 보고 알맞은 문장에 ✓ 표시를 하세요.

1

- [ ] The kitten likes to jump and run.
- [ ] The kitten likes to play with string.

2

- [ ] I found a kitten in my backyard.
- [ ] I found a kitten under a bench.

3

- [ ] The kitten slept on the sofa.
- [ ] The kitten sat on my lap.

C 다음 문장이 옳으면 T(True), 틀리면 F(False)에 동그라미 하세요.

1 The kitten was hiding in a bush. T F

2 Mom named the kitten Milo. T F

3 They put up the poster at the park. T F

D 빈칸을 채워 이야기 순서에 맞게 문장을 완성하세요.

I found a ________ in my backyard.
I named the kitten ________.

We ________ a poster: "Is This Your Cat?"

A lady said, "That's my kitten!"
She came and took Milo ________.

I visited Milo at his house.
He sat on my ________ and purred.

lap	Milo	kitten	made	home

Think & Say

이 글에서 상황에 따라 아이의 감정은 어떻게 달라졌을까요?

1. The girl finds a lost kitten. ☐ worried ☐ angry
2. The kitten goes back to the lady. ☐ bored ☐ sad
3. The girl visits the kitten and sees he is safe. ☐ happy ☐ worried

Listen Again

● 스토리를 다시 들으며 빈칸에 알맞은 단어를 써 넣으세요. (29)

[April 1] Today, I found a kitten in my ________. It was hiding in a bush. It was small and ________. Mom said, "Let's help the ________ kitten."

[April 3] I ________d the kitten Milo. Milo likes to play with ________. We made a ________: "Is This Your Cat?" We put it up at the park.

[April 7] A lady called about Milo. She said, "That's my ________!" She came and took Milo home. I was sad to say good-bye but happy Milo found his ________.

[April 10] I ________ed Milo at his house. He sat on my lap and ________ed. The lady said, "Thank you for saving him." "I'm so glad he is back home," I smiled.

purr
kitten
family
name
backyard
lost
poster
string
gray
visit

Sentence Patterns

● 다음 필수 문형을 다양한 예문에 적용해 보세요. (30)

1 I found ______ in ______ . 나는 ~을 …에서 찾았어요.

❶ 나는 아기 고양이를 뒷마당에서 찾았어요.

I found a kitten in my backyard.

❷ 나는 개구리를 연못에서 찾았어요.

I found ______ in ______ .

❸ 나는 달팽이를 정원에서 찾았어요.

I found ______ in ______ .

2 I named ______ ______ . 나는 ~을 …라고 이름 지었어요.

❶ 나는 그 아기 고양이를 마일로라고 이름 지었어요.

I named the kitten Milo.

❷ 나는 그 개를 맥스라고 이름 지었어요.

I named ______ ______ .

❸ 나는 그 물고기를 골디라고 이름 지었어요.

I named ______ ______ .

Word Box

- leave my friend 내 친구와 헤어지다
- the fish, Goldie 그 물고기, 골디
- lose the game 경기에서 지다
- a snail, the garden 달팽이, 정원
- a frog, the pond 개구리, 연못
- the dog, Max 그 개, 맥스

3 I was sad to ______ . 나는 ~해서 슬펐어요.

① 나는 작별 인사를 해서 슬펐어요.

I was sad to say good-bye.

② 나는 경기에서 져서 슬펐어요.

I was sad to ______.

③ 나는 내 친구와 헤어져서 슬펐어요.

I was sad to ______.

Try Writing

배운 필수 문형을 활용해 영작해 보세요.

1 나는 공을 공원에서 찾았어요. (a ball, the park)

______

2 나는 그 거북을 스피디라고 이름 지었어요. (the turtle, Speedy)

______

3 나는 그 소식을 들어서 슬펐어요. (hear the news)

______

Think More

Found Cat

★ 고양이 주인을 찾는 포스터를 만들었어요. 길 잃은 고양이를 찾아 ✓ 표시를 하세요.

Is This Your Cat?

I found this cat near Maple Park
on August 15.
It has short brown fur.
It has black stripes on its legs.

?

Please call Stella: 010-111-1234

• fur 털 stripe 줄무늬

Plus 길을 잃은 동물이 보호자를 찾지 못하면 동물 보호소에 보내지기도 해요. 동물 보호소는 깨끗한 먹이와 잠자리를 마련해 주며 동물을 안전하게 돌봐줘요. 동물에게 이름표나 마이크로칩이 있다면 보호소에서 확인해 가족을 찾아줄 수 있어요. 만약 주인을 찾지 못하면, 보호소는 새로운 가족을 만나게 해 주기도 해요.

Unit 7

The Pumpkin Growing Contest

STEP 1 읽기 핵심 단어를 익혀서 스토리 듣고 읽기

STEP 2 이해 읽은 내용을 점검하여 스토리 이해하기

STEP 3 확장 필수 문형 학습으로 문장 이해력 키우기

Key Words

• 다음 단어들을 하나씩 손으로 짚으며 잘 들어 보세요. 31

pumpkin

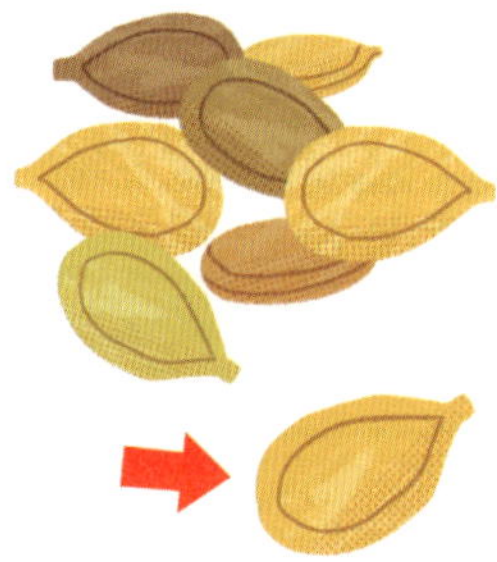

seed

plant

grow

sprout

leaf

leaves 잎들

cucumber

show

온라인 단어 학습

온라인 학습으로 단어를 꼼꼼히 익혀요.

A 단어와 우리말 뜻을 알맞게 연결하세요.

1	sprout	싹이 나다, 새싹
2	grow	호박
3	pumpkin	씨
4	seed	기르다, 자라다

B 다음 우리말 뜻에 맞는 단어를 찾아 동그라미 하고 한 번 쓰세요.

g	s	h	o	w	e	s	b
p	j	o	r	t	l	y	n
l	u	k	z	h	e	m	i
a	f	m	d	u	a	c	g
n	r	p	i	a	f	w	k
t	x	s	g	y	o	t	q
c	u	c	u	m	b	e	r
h	d	v	l	w	j	r	f

1 오이

c

2 잎

l

3 (씨앗 등을) 심다, 식물

p

4 보여주다

s

The Pumpkin Growing Contest

Jack's class had a pumpkin growing contest.

Everyone in his class planted pumpkin seeds.

Jack said, "**I can't wait to** grow a big pumpkin!"

contest 대회 | can't wait to ~하고 싶다, ~가 기대된다

He watered the seeds every day.

A few days later, the seeds sprouted.

Jack's sprout grew fast.

But the leaves didn't look like pumpkin leaves.

water 물을 주다 | look like ~처럼 보이다

Jack watched his plant carefully.

One day, small flowers came out.

Then, a cucumber **started to** grow!

cucumber seeds

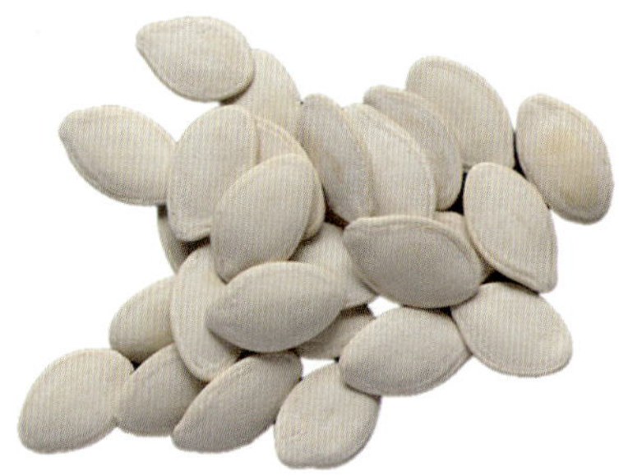

pumpkin seeds

come out (꽃이) 피다 (과거형 came out)

It was time to show the plants.

Everyone brought their pumpkins.

"I grew this!" Jack said.

The class laughed and clapped.

"That's the best cucumber ever!" Ms. Green said.

bring 가져오다 (과거형 brought) | clap 박수를 치다

Comprehension

A 보기에서 알맞은 단어를 골라 빈칸에 쓰세요.

pumpkin sprout grow cucumber flower

1 

One day, small ______s came out.

2 

"That's the best ______ ever!" Ms. Green said.

3 

A few days later, the seeds ______ed.

4 

But the leaves didn't look like ______ leaves.

5 

"I can't wait to ______ a big pumpkin!"

B 그림을 보고 알맞은 문장에 ✓ 표시를 하세요.

1 

- ☐ Everyone planted pumpkin seeds.
- ☐ Everyone watered the flowers.

2 

- ☐ A pumpkin started to grow!
- ☐ A cucumber started to grow!

3 

- ☐ Everyone brought their pumpkins.
- ☐ The class laughed and clapped.

C 다음 문장이 옳으면 T(True), 틀리면 F(False)에 동그라미 하세요.

1 Jack's class had a cucumber growing contest. T F

2 Jack watered his seeds every day. T F

3 Jack showed his pumpkin to the class. T F

D 이야기 순서에 맞는 문장을 찾아 각 그림에 알맞은 기호를 쓰세요.

ⓐ Jack's sprout grew fast.

ⓑ The leaves didn't look like pumpkin leaves.

ⓒ Jack showed his cucumber to the class.

ⓓ Everyone in Jack's class planted pumpkin seeds.

Think & Say

식물이 잘 자라게 하려면 어떻게 해야 할까요? 알맞은 답을 모두 고르세요.

- ☐ Give it water. (물을 주세요.)
- ☐ Put it in a dark place. (어두운 곳에 두세요.)
- ☐ Use good soil. (좋은 흙을 사용하세요.)
- ☐ Give it sunlight. (햇빛을 주세요.)

Listen Again

● 스토리를 다시 들으며 빈칸에 알맞은 단어를 써 넣으세요. 34

Jack's class had a pumpkin growing contest. Everyone in his class ________ed pumpkin seeds. Jack said, "I can't wait to grow a big ________!"

He watered the ________s every day. A few days later, the seeds ________ed. Jack's sprout grew fast. But the ________ didn't look like pumpkin leaves.

Jack watched his plant carefully. One day, small ________s came out. Then, a cucumber started to ________!

It was time to ________ the plants. Everyone brought their pumpkins. "I grew this!" Jack said. The class laughed and ________ped. "That's the best ________ ever!" Ms. Green said.

clap
flower
show
plant
seed
grow
pumpkin
sprout
leaves
cucumber

Sentence Patterns

● 다음 필수 문형을 다양한 예문에 적용해 보세요. (35)

1 I can't wait to ______ ! ~하는 게 너무 기다려져요!

① 호박을 키우는 게 너무 기다려져요!

I can't wait to grow a pumpkin !

② 케이크를 굽는 게 너무 기다려져요!

I can't wait to ______ !

③ 눈사람을 만드는 게 너무 기다려져요!

I can't wait to ______ !

2 ______ started to ______ . ~가 …하기 시작했어요.

① 오이 하나가 자라기 시작했어요.

A cucumber started to grow .

② 아기가 울기 시작했어요.

______ started to ______ .

③ 내 아이스크림이 녹기 시작했어요.

______ started to ______ .

Word Box

- my ice cream, melt 내 아이스크림, 녹다
- feed the dog 개에게 먹이를 주다
- bake a cake 케이크를 굽다
- make a snowman 눈사람을 만들다
- wash the dishes 설거지를 하다
- the baby, cry 아기, 울다

3 It was time to ______ . ~할 시간이었어요.

① 식물을 보여줄 시간이었어요.

It was time to show the plants .

② 개에게 먹이를 줄 시간이었어요.

It was time to ______ .

③ 설거지를 할 시간이었어요.

It was time to ______ .

Try Writing

배운 필수 문형을 활용해 영작해 보세요.

1

내 가방을 쌀 시간이었어요. (pack my bag)

______

2

나뭇잎들이 떨어지기 시작했어요. (the leaves, fall)

______

3

축구를 하는 게 너무 기다려져요! (play soccer)

______

Think More

From Seed to Pumpkin

★ 호박의 성장 단계에 맞도록 빈칸에 알맞은 단어를 찾아 쓰세요.

① A pumpkin grows from a ____________.

② A seed ____________s.

③ The plant grows a long vine.

④ Yellow ____________s appear.

⑤ A green pumpkin grows.

⑥ The green pumpkin turns ____________.

flower　　orange　　sprout　　seed

• vine 넝쿨

Plus 꽃은 열매와 씨앗을 만들기 위해 꼭 필요해요. 하지만 혼자서는 어렵기 때문에 곤충의 도움을 받아요. 벌이나 나비가 꿀을 먹으러 꽃에 오면 꽃가루가 묻어서 다른 꽃으로 옮겨 가요. 이것을 '수분'이라고 해요. 수분이 되어야 씨앗이 생기고 열매가 맺혀요. 곤충이 없다면 많은 식물이 열매를 만들지 못하게 돼요.

Unit 8

Saving Sea Animals

STEP 1 읽기 핵심 단어를 익혀서 스토리 듣고 읽기

STEP 2 이해 읽은 내용을 점검하여 스토리 이해하기

STEP 3 확장 필수 문형 학습으로 문장 이해력 키우기

Key Words

- 다음 단어들을 하나씩 손으로 짚으며 잘 들어 보세요. 36

온라인 단어 학습

온라인 학습으로 단어를 꼼꼼히 익혀요.

A 단어와 우리말 뜻을 알맞게 연결하세요.

1	stuck	그물
2	net	기름
3	oil	~에 끼어 꼼짝 못하는
4	seal	바다표범

B 우리말 뜻에 맞는 단어가 되도록 빈칸에 알맞은 글자를 쓰세요.

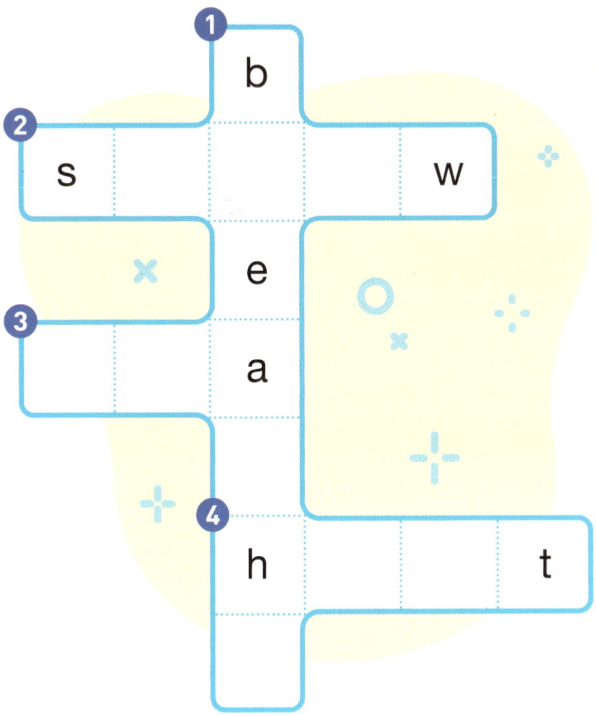

1 숨을 쉬다

2 빨대

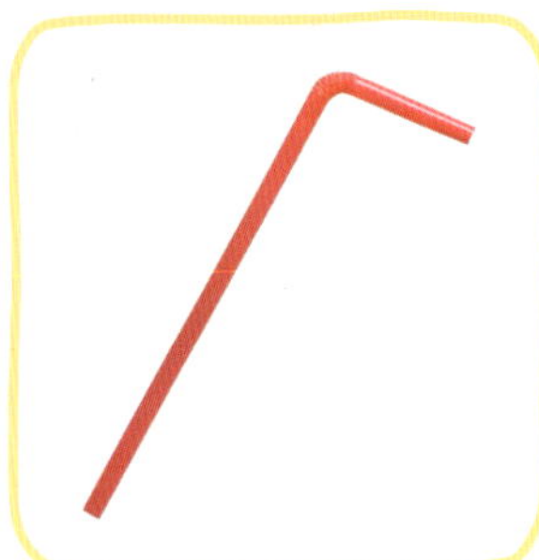

3 바다

4 다치게 하다, 다친

Saving Sea Animals

There is too much trash in the sea.

It hurts sea animals.

Our Sea Animal Rescue Center helps the hurt animals.

trash 쓰레기 | rescue 구조

A plastic bag was stuck on a penguin's head.

It couldn't breathe well.

We carefully took the bag off.

A sharp straw was stuck in a turtle's nose.

We gently took it out.

plastic bag 비닐봉지 | sharp 날카로운 |
gentl‍y 부드럽게 | take out 꺼내다 (과거형 took out)

A dolphin swam through an oil spill.

The oil covered its skin.

We cleaned the dolphin and kept it safe.

A seal got tangled in a fishing net.

It couldn't get out.

We cut the net and set it free.

swim 수영하다 (과거형 swam) | cover 덮다 | skin 피부 | clean 닦다 | tangled 뒤얽힌 | set free ~를 자유롭게 하다

We must not throw trash into the sea.

Then, sea animals can live safely.

Let's help keep the sea clean!

must not ~하면 안 된다 | throw 던지다

Comprehension

A 보기에서 알맞은 단어를 골라 빈칸에 쓰세요.

trash   net   dolphin   sea   breathe

1 

There is too much ______ in the sea.

2 

A ______ swam through an oil spill.

3 

A seal got tangled in a fishing ______ .

4 

A penguin couldn't ______ well.

5 

We must not throw trash into the ______ .

B 그림을 보고 알맞은 문장에 ✓ 표시를 하세요.

1 

- [ ] They throw trash into the sea.
- [ ] They help keep the sea clean.

2 

- [ ] Too much trash hurts sea animals.
- [ ] Sea animals live safely.

3 

- [ ] The oil covered a dolphin's skin.
- [ ] The seal couldn't get out.

C 다음 문장이 옳으면 T(True), 틀리면 F(False)에 동그라미 하세요.

1 There is too much trash in the sea. T F

2 A turtle had a plastic bag on its head. T F

3 They took the hurt sea animals to the zoo. T F

D 위험에 빠진 동물들에게 일어난 일과 해결 방법을 정리해 보세요.

Problem(문제)		Solution(해결)
• A ______ was stuck on a penguin's head.		• We carefully took the bag off.
• A sharp straw was stuck in a turtle's nose.		• We gently took out the ______.
• A dolphin swam through an ______ spill.		• We cleaned the dolphin and kept it safe.
• A seal got tangled in a fishing net.		• We cut the ______ and set the seal free.

straw oil net plastic bag

Think & Say

위험에 처한 거북이 말을 할 수 있다면, 어떤 말을 하고 싶을까요?
알맞은 말을 모두 골라 보세요.

☐ Help me. ☐ Let's swim together.

☐ It's sunny today. ☐ Keep the sea clean.

Listen Again

● 스토리를 다시 들으며 빈칸에 알맞은 단어를 써 넣으세요. 39

There is too much trash in the ______. It hurts sea animals. Our Sea Animal Rescue Center helps the ______ animals.

A plastic bag was ______ on a penguin's head. It couldn't ______ well. We carefully took the bag off.

A sharp ______ was stuck in a turtle's nose. We gently took it out.

A dolphin swam through an ______ spill. The oil covered its skin. We cleaned the dolphin and kept it safe.

A ______ got tangled in a fishing net. It couldn't get out. We cut the ______ and set it free.

We must not throw ______ into the sea. Then, sea animals can live safely. Let's help keep the sea ______!

oil
trash
sea
hurt
breathe
clean
seal
net
straw
stuck

Sentence Patterns

● 다음 필수 문형을 다양한 예문에 적용해 보세요. 40

1 There is too much ______ in ______ . …에 ~가 너무 많아요.

❶ 바다에 쓰레기가 너무 많아요.

There is too much trash in the sea.

❷ 공기 중에 먼지가 너무 많아요.

There is too much ______ in ______ .

❸ 거리에 소음이 너무 많아요.

There is too much ______ in ______ .

2 It couldn't ______ . 그것은 ~할 수 없었어요.

❶ 그것은 숨을 잘 쉴 수 없었어요.

It couldn't breathe well.

❷ 그것은 빠르게 움직일 수 없었어요.

It couldn't ______ .

❸ 그것은 높이 뛸 수 없었어요.

It couldn't ______ .

Word Box

- noise, the street 소음, 거리
- move fast 빠르게 움직이다
- make noise 떠들다
- waste water 물을 낭비하다
- dust, the air 먼지, 공기
- jump high 높이 뛰다

3 We must not ______ . 우리는 ~하면 안 돼요.

❶ 우리는 바다에 쓰레기를 버리면 안 돼요.

We must not throw trash into the sea.

❷ 우리는 물을 낭비하면 안 돼요.

We must not ______________________.

❸ 우리는 떠들면 안 돼요.

We must not ______________________.

Try Writing

배운 필수 문형을 활용해 영작해 보세요.

1 

그것은 빠르게 수영할 수 없었어요. (swim fast)

____

2 

우리는 돌을 던지면 안 돼요. (throw rocks)

____

3 

도시에 차량이 너무 많아요. (traffic, the city)

____

Think More

Save the Ocean

★ 바다를 지키기 위해 우리가 어떤 노력을 해야 할까요?
옳은 문장은 ○, 틀린 문장은 ×에 표시하세요.

O X We should throw trash into the sea.

O X We should use more plastic.

O X We should recycle bottles and cans.

O X We should pick up trash at the beach.

O X We should protect sea animals in the ocean.

O X We should try not to use plastic straws.

pick up 줍다 ocean 대양, 바다

Plus 거북은 비닐봉지를 해파리로 착각해 먹기도 해요. 하지만 비닐이 몸 속에서 소화되지 않아 제대로 먹지 못해 결국 죽고 말아요. 바다표범은 바다에 버려진 그물이나 밧줄에 몸이 걸려 상처를 입거나 물 밖으로 숨 쉬러 나오지 못해 목숨을 잃기도 해요. 이처럼 작은 쓰레기 하나가 바다 동물들에게 큰 고통이 될 수 있어요.

Review Test 2
(Unit ⑤ – Unit ⑧)

/ 25개

A 그림에 알맞은 단어를 고르세요.

1 

ⓐ call　ⓑ grow　ⓒ fight

2 

ⓐ decide　ⓑ choose　ⓒ hide

3 

ⓐ plant　ⓑ hurt　ⓒ breathe

4 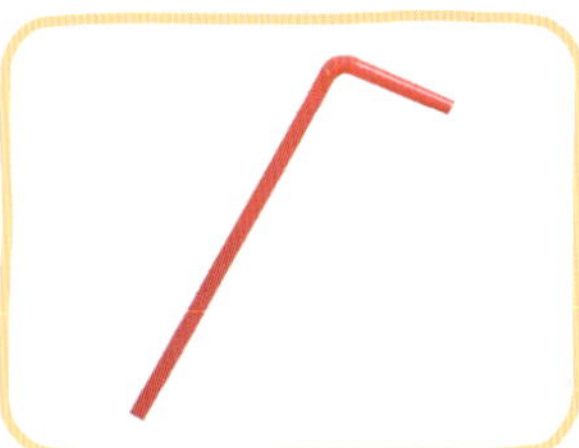

ⓐ finger　ⓑ straw　ⓒ string

5 

ⓐ leaf　ⓑ seed　ⓒ sprout

6 

ⓐ movie　ⓑ seal　ⓒ sea

B 그림을 보고 알맞은 문장을 고르세요.

1 

ⓐ They look at the movie posters.

ⓑ They buy some popcorn.

2 

ⓐ I was sad to say good-bye.

ⓑ I found a kitten in my backyard.

3 

ⓐ A pumpkin started to grow!

ⓑ Small flowers came out.

4 

ⓐ A plastic bag was stuck on its head.

ⓑ It got tangled in a fishing net.

★★
C 알맞은 단어를 골라 문장을 완성하세요.

1 I can't wait to ⓐ grow ⓑ growing a big pumpkin!

2 It ⓐ were ⓑ was hiding in a bush.

3 Emma and her friends ⓐ go ⓑ goes to the movies.

4 A sharp straw was stuck in a ⓐ turtle ⓑ turtle's nose.

D 짧은 글을 읽고 질문에 알맞은 대답을 고르세요.

1 빈칸에 들어갈 알맞은 단어를 고르세요.

Emma chooses the animal movie.
"The animals go on a trip together.
It looks __________," she says.

ⓐ exciting

ⓑ sad

2 빈칸에 들어갈 알맞은 단어를 고르세요.

Jack planted pumpkin seeds. He watered the seeds every day. A few days later, the __________ sprouted.

ⓐ seeds

ⓑ fruits

3 밑줄 친 poster에 들어갈 알맞은 제목을 고르세요.

I found a kitten in my backyard.
I made a <u>poster</u> to help the lost kitten.
I put it up at the park.

ⓐ That's My Kitten!

ⓑ Is This Your Cat?

4 빈칸에 들어갈 알맞은 문장을 고르세요.

____
Then, sea animals can live safely.
Let's help keep the sea clean!

ⓐ We must not throw trash into the sea.

ⓑ We must not use plastic.

E 필수 패턴을 활용해 우리말에 알맞은 영어 문장을 완성하세요.

I can't wait to ______ !	It was time to ______ .
They talk about ______ .	We must not ______ .

1 개에게 먹이를 줄 시간이었어요.

→ ______________________ feed the dog.

2 그들은 어느 버스를 탈지에 대해 이야기해요.

→ ______________________ which bus to take.

3 눈사람을 만드는 게 너무 기다려져요!

→ ______________________ make a snowman!

4 우리는 물을 낭비하면 안 돼요.

→ ______________________ waste water.

F 우리말에 알맞은 영어 문장을 쓰세요.

1 말하는 앵무새들이 있어요. (are, parrots, talking, there)

→ ______________________________________.

2 그것은 빠르게 움직일 수 없었어요. (fast, move, couldn't, it)

→ ______________________________________.

3 나는 경기에서 져서 슬펐어요. (was, the game, I, sad, to lose)

→ ______________________________________.

B권이 끝났습니다.
C권으로 넘어갈까요?

저자 C2 Archive (대표 Olene Kim)

지난 20여 년간 영어라는 언어를 어린이들이 어려움 없이 단계적으로 습득해갈 수 있도록
효과적인 교수법을 연구하여 다양한 교재로 구현해 온 영어교육 전문 집필진입니다.
파닉스, 리딩, 코스북, 문법 등 여러 분야의 ELT 교재와 영어 단행본 학습서를 집필·개발하였습니다.

저자 기적학습연구소

"혼자서 작은 산을 넘는 아이가 나중에 큰 산도 넘습니다." 본 연구소는 아이들이 혼자서 큰 산까지
넘을 수 있는 힘을 키워주고자 합니다. 아이들의 연령에 맞게 학습의 산을 작게 만들어 혼자서도
쉽게 넘을 수 있게 만듭니다. 때로는 작은 고난도 경험하게 하여 성취감도 맛보게 합니다.
그리고 아이들에게 실제로 적용해서 검증을 통해 차근차근 책을 만듭니다.

기적의 영어리딩 Level 3B

Miracle Series – Reading English

초판 발행 • 2025년 11월 15일

지은이 • C2 Archive, 기적학습연구소

발행인 • 이종원
발행처 • (주)길벗스쿨
출판사 등록일 • 2025년 5월 28일 | **주소** • 서울시 마포구 월드컵로 10길 56(서교동)
대표 전화 • 02)332-0931 | **팩스** • 02)310-4700
홈페이지 • www.gilbutschool.co.kr | **이메일** • gilbut@gilbut.co.kr

담당편집 • 김소이(soykim@gilbut.co.kr), 이경희, 김예지 | **기획** • 이경희, 김남희, 박민혜 | **표지디자인** • 이현숙 | **제작** • 손일순
영업마케팅 • 문세연, 박선경, 구혜지, 박다슬 | **웹마케팅** • 박달님, 이재윤, 이지수, 나혜연 | **영업관리** • 정경화 | **독자지원** • 윤정아

교정교열 • 최주연 | **전산편집** • 기본기획 | **본문디자인** • 신세진 | **삽화** • 김수영, 삼식이, 엄수지, 윤지현, 이탁근, 조은, 최선화, Bananabee | **영문 감수** • Ryan P. Lagace
인쇄 및 제본 • 영림 | **녹음** • 아람 멀티미디어

Photo Credits
해당 이미지는 Shutterstock.com의 라이선스 하에 사용되었습니다.
p.47 (Dmitrii Iakimov)

ISBN 979-11-7467-058-8 64740 (길벗 도서번호 30637)
정가 17,000원

제 품 명 : 기적의 영어리딩 3B
제조사명 : (주)길벗스쿨
제조국명 : 대한민국
전화번호 : 02-332-0931
주　　소 : 서울시 마포구 월드컵로 10길 56 (서교동)
제조년월 : 판권에 별도 표기
사용연령 : **8세 이상**
KC마크는 이 제품이 공통안전기준에 적합하였음을 의미합니다.

기적 영어 학습서

기본이 탄탄! 실전에서 척척!
유초등 필수 영어능력을 길러주는 코어 학습서

유아 영어

재미있는 액티비티가 가득한
4~6세를 위한 영어 워크북

- 4세 이상
- 5세 이상
- 6세 이상
- 6세 이상

파닉스 완성 프로그램

알파벳 음가 ➜ 사이트워드
➜ 읽기 연습까지!
리딩을 위한 탄탄한 기초 만들기

- 6세 이상 전 3권
- 1~3학년
- 1~3학년 전 3권

영어 단어

영어 실력의 가장 큰 바탕은 어휘력!
교과과정 필수 어휘 익히기

- 3학년 이상 전 2권
- 1~2학년 전 2권
- 3~4학년 전 2권
- 5~6학년 전 2권

영어 리딩

패턴 문장 리딩으로 시작해
정확한 해석을 위한 끊어 읽기까지!
탄탄한 독해 실력 쌓기

- 2~3학년 전 3권
- 3~4학년 전 3권
- 4~5학년 전 2권
- 5~6학년 전 2권
- 5~6학년 전 2권

영어 라이팅

저학년은 패턴 영작으로,
고학년은 5형식 문장 만들기 연습으로
튼튼한 영작 실력 완성

- 2학년 이상 전 4권
- 4학년 이상 전 5권
- 5학년 이상 전 2권
- 6학년 이상

영어일기

한 줄 쓰기부터 생활일기,
주제일기까지!
영어 글쓰기 실력을 키우는 시리즈

- 3학년 이상
- 4~5학년
- 5~6학년

영문법

중학 영어 대비, 영어 구사
정확성을 키워주는 영문법 학습

- 4~5학년 전 2권
- 5~6학년 전 3권
- 6학년 이상

초등 필수 영어 무작정 따라하기

초등 시기에 놓쳐서는 안 될 필수 학습은 바로 영어 교과서!
영어 교과서 5종의 핵심 내용을 쏙쏙 뽑아 한 권으로 압축 정리했습니다.
초등 과정의 필수학습으로 기초를 다져서 중학교 및 상위 학습의 단단한 토대가 되게 합니다.

1~2학년

2~3학년

2~3학년

3학년 이상

4학년 이상

미국교과서 리딩

문제의 차이가 영어 실력의 차이! 논픽션 리딩에 강해지는 《미국교과서 READING》
논픽션 리딩에 가장 좋은 재료인 미국 교과과정의 주제를 담은 지문을 읽고, 독해력과
문제 해결력을 두루 향상시킬 수 있도록 구성한 단계별 리딩 프로그램

LEVEL 1

준비 단계

LEVEL 2

시작 단계

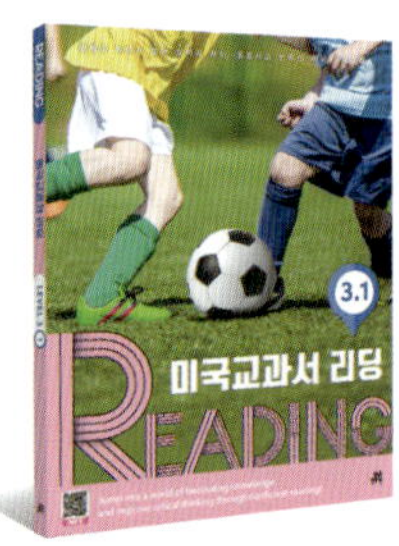

LEVEL 3

정독 연습 단계

LEVEL 4

독해 정확성 향상 단계

LEVEL 5

독해 통합심화 단계

3B

90~110 words
AR 1.3~2.3

기적의 영어리딩

with 문장 패턴

Practice Book

(정답과 해석 포함)

길벗스쿨

3B

기적의 영어리딩

Practice Book

Unit 1 Ride Safely

READ AND WRITE 문장을 의미 단위로 나눠 읽은 뒤, 전체 문장을 따라 쓰세요.

1 나는 자전거 타는 것을 아주 좋아해요.

I	love	riding my bike.
나는	아주 좋아한다	자전거를 타는 것을

2 안전하게 지내려면, 몇 가지 규칙을 따라야 해요.

To stay safe,	we	have to	follow	some rules.
안전하게 지내려면	우리는	~해야 한다	따른다	몇 가지 규칙들을

3 나는 항상 헬멧을 써요.

I	always	wear	a helmet.
나는	항상	쓴다	헬멧을

4 나는 도로가 아니라 자전거 전용 도로에서 타요.

I ride	in the bike lane,	not on the road.
나는 탄다	자전거 전용 도로에서	(차가 다니는) 도로가 아니라

5 나는 사람들을 치지 않도록 조심해요.

I	am careful	not to hit	people.
나는	조심한다	치지 않도록	사람들을

6 나는 초록불로 바뀔 때까지 기다려요.

I wait 나는 기다린다	until ~할 때까지	it turns 그것이 변한다	green. 초록불로

7 빠르게 가면 위험할 수 있어요!

Going fast 빠르게 가는 것은	can be ~일 수 있다	dangerous! 위험한

8 젖은 길은 미끄러울 수 있어요.

Wet roads 젖은 길은	can be ~일 수 있다	slippery. 미끄러운

9 내 남동생도 자전거를 타고 싶어 해요.

My little brother 내 남동생은	wants 원한다	to ride, 자전거 타기를	too. 또한

10 너에게 맞는 크기의 자전거를 골라.

Choose 골라라	the right size bike 맞는 크기의 자전거를	for you. 너에게 맞는

Unit 2 My Summer Vacation

READ AND WRITE 문장을 의미 단위로 나눠 읽은 뒤, 전체 문장을 따라 쓰세요.

1 여름 방학이 오늘 시작됐어요.

Summer vacation	began	today.
여름 방학이	시작됐다	오늘

2 나는 하루 종일 친구들과 놀았어요.

I	played	with my friends	all day.
나는	놀았다	친구들과	하루 종일

3 하루 계획표를 만드는 게 어때?

How about	making	a daily schedule?
~하는 게 어때?	만드는 것	하루 계획표를

4 나는 앉아서 하루 계획표를 써요.

I	sit and write	my daily schedule.
나는	앉아서 쓴다	내 하루 계획표를

5 하지만 내게는 지루해 보여요.

But	it looks	boring	to me.
하지만	그것은 ~해 보인다	지루한	나에게

6 다음 날, 나는 내 계획표를 지키려고 노력했어요.

The next day,	I tried	to follow my schedule.
다음 날	나는 노력했다	내 계획표를 지키려고

7 나는 7시에 일어났지만 다시 잠들었어요.

I woke up	at 7,	but	I fell asleep	again.
나는 일어났다	7시에	하지만	나는 잠들었다	다시

8 나는 재미로 컴퓨터 게임을 하기 시작했어요.

I started	playing computer games	for fun.
나는 시작했다	컴퓨터 게임을 하는 것을	재미로

9 자기 전에 아직 줄넘기를 할 수 있잖아!

You	can still	jump rope	before bed!
너는	아직 ~할 수 있다	줄넘기를 한다	자기 전에

10 오늘 계획 중에 한 가지는 했어!

I did	one thing	on my schedule	today!
나는 했다	한 가지를	내 계획에서	오늘

Unit 3 The Rainy Barbecue

READ AND WRITE 문장을 의미 단위로 나눠 읽은 뒤, 전체 문장을 따라 쓰세요.

1 하루 종일 맑을 거야.

It'll be ~일 것이다	sunny 화창한	all day. 하루 종일

2 그들은 그릴을 설치했어요.

They 그들은	set up 설치했다	the grill. 그릴을

3 아빠는 바비큐를 하려고 불을 붙였어요.

Dad 아빠는	lit the fire 불을 붙였다	for the barbecue. 바비큐를 하려고

4 갑자기 강한 바람이 불었어요.

Suddenly, 갑자기	a strong wind 강한 바람이	blew. 불었다

5 불이 꺼지고, 엄마의 스카프가 날아가 버렸어요!

The fire 불이	went out, 꺼졌다	and Mom's scarf 그리고 엄마의 스카프가	flew away! 날아가 버렸다

6 검은 구름이 하늘에 나타났어요.

Dark clouds 검은 구름들이	appeared 나타났다	in the sky. 하늘에

7 내가 어제 일기 예보를 봤어!

I 나는	looked at 봤다	yesterday's forecast! 어제의 일기 예보를

8 비가 쏟아지고, 바람이 더 거세졌어요.

It poured, 비가 쏟아졌다	and the wind 그리고 바람이	grew stronger. 더 거세졌다

9 엄마는 샌드위치를 꺼냈어요.

Mom 엄마는	took out 꺼냈다	our sandwiches. 우리의 샌드위치를

10 빗속에서 소풍을 하는 것이 재미있네.

It's fun ~은 재미있다	to have a picnic 소풍을 하는 것	in the rain. 빗속에서

Unit 4 The Flying Helpers

READ AND WRITE 문장을 의미 단위로 나눠 읽은 뒤, 전체 문장을 따라 쓰세요.

1 드론 센터에는 전화가 많이 와요.

The Drone Center	gets	many calls.
드론 센터는	받는다	많은 전화를

2 사람들은 하늘을 나는 도움 요원들이 필요해요.

People	need	flying helpers.
사람들은	필요하다	하늘을 나는 도움 요원들이

3 드론들이 도울 준비가 되어 있어요!

Drones	are ready	to help!
드론들은	준비가 되어 있다	도울

4 그것은 들판 위를 날아요.

It	flies	over a field.
그것은	난다	들판 위를

5 농작물이 건강한지를 점검해요.

It	checks	if	the crops are healthy.
그것은	점검한다	~인지 아닌지	농작물이 건강하다

6 위험에 처한 사람들을 찾을 수 있어요.

It 그것은	can find 찾을 수 있다	people 사람들을	in danger. 위험에 처한

7 금이 간 곳이나 다른 문제들을 찾아요.

It 그것은	looks for ~을 찾는다	cracks 금이 간 곳들을	or other problems. 혹은 다른 문제들을

8 야생동물들을 놀라게 하지 않고 지켜봐요.

It 그것은	watches 지켜본다	wild animals 야생동물들을	without scaring them. 그들을 놀라게 하지 않고

9 아마도 가까운 미래에는 드론 택시가 생길 거예요.

Maybe 아마도	we 우리는	will have 가지게 될 것이다	drone taxis 드론 택시를	in the near future. 가까운 미래에

10 도로 위를 날 수 있어요.

You 당신은	could fly 날 수 있다	above the roads. 도로 위를

Unit 5 Pick a Movie!

READ AND WRITE 문장을 의미 단위로 나눠 읽은 뒤, 전체 문장을 따라 쓰세요.

1 그들은 영화 포스터들을 봐요.

They 그들은	look at ~을 본다	the movie posters. 영화 포스터들을

2 그들은 어떤 영화를 볼지 이야기해요.

They 그들은	talk about ~에 대해 이야기한다	which movie to see. 어떤 영화를 볼지

3 잭은 슈퍼히어로 영화를 보고 싶어해요.

Jack 잭은	wants 원한다	to see 보는 것을	the superhero movie. 슈퍼히어로 영화를

4 그들은 악당들과 싸우고 사람들을 도와요.

They 그들은	fight bad guys 악당들과 싸운다	and 그리고	help people. 사람들을 돕는다

5 그는 슈퍼히어로처럼 손을 내밀어요.

He 그는	holds out 내민다	his hand 그의 손을	like a superhero. 슈퍼히어로처럼

6 하늘을 나는 책들과 말하는 모자들이 있어요.

There are ~가 있다	flying books 하늘을 나는 책들	and talking hats. 그리고 말하는 모자들

7 이야기는 놀라움으로 가득할 거야!

The story 그 이야기는	will be full of ~로 가득할 것이다	surprises! 놀라움

8 소피아는 마법사처럼 손가락을 흔들어요.

Sophia 소피아는	waves 흔든다	her finger 그녀의 손가락을	like a wizard. 마법사처럼

9 동물들이 함께 여행을 가.

The animals 동물들은	go on a trip 여행을 간다	together. 함께

10 결정하기 어려워.

It's hard 어렵다	to decide. 결정하는 것은

Unit 6 The Lost Kitten

READ AND WRITE 문장을 의미 단위로 나눠 읽은 뒤, 전체 문장을 따라 쓰세요.

1 오늘 나는 뒷마당에서 아기 고양이를 발견했어요.

Today,	I	found	a kitten	in my backyard.
오늘	나는	발견했다	아기 고양이를	뒷마당에서

2 그것은 덤불 속에 숨어 있었어요.

It	was hiding	in a bush.
그것은 (= 아기 고양이는)	숨어 있었다	덤불 속에

3 나는 아기 고양이에게 '마일로'라고 이름을 지었어요.

I	named	the kitten	Milo.
나는	이름을 지었다	아기 고양이를	'마일로'라고

4 마일로는 줄 가지고 노는 것을 좋아해요.

Milo	likes	to play with string.
마일로는	좋아한다	줄 가지고 노는 것을

5 우리는 그것을 공원에 붙였어요.

We	put it up	at the park.
우리는	그것을 붙였다	공원에

6 그분은 와서 마일로를 집으로 데려갔어요.

She 그녀는	came and took 와서 데려갔다	Milo 마일로를	home. 집으로

7 나는 작별 인사를 해서 슬펐지만, 마일로가 가족을 찾아서 기뻤어요.

I was sad 나는 슬펐다	to say good-bye 작별 인사를 해서	but happy 하지만 기뻤다	Milo found his family. 마일로가 그의 가족을 찾아서

8 나는 마일로의 집에 방문했다.

I 나는	visited 방문했다	Milo 마일로를	at his house. 그의 집에서

9 그는 내 무릎에 앉아서 가르랑거렸어요.

He 그는 (= 마일로는)	sat 앉았다	on my lap 내 무릎에	and purred. 그리고 가르랑거렸다

10 그를 구해줘서 고마워요.

Thank you 고맙다	for saving 구해줘서	him. 그를 (= 아기 고양이를)

Unit 7 The Pumpkin Growing Contest

READ AND WRITE 문장을 의미 단위로 나눠 읽은 뒤, 전체 문장을 따라 쓰세요.

1 잭의 반에서 호박 키우기 대회를 열었어요.

Jack's class 잭의 반은	had 열었다	a pumpkin growing contest. 호박 키우기 대회를

2 그의 반 친구들 모두 호박씨를 심었어요.

Everyone in his class 그의 반 모두가	planted 심었다	pumpkin seeds. 호박씨를

3 나는 큰 호박을 키우는 게 너무 기다려져요!

I can't wait 나는 기다릴 수 없다 (= 너무 기다려진다)	to grow 키우는 것을	a big pumpkin! 큰 호박을

4 그는 매일 씨앗들에 물을 주었어요.

He 그는	watered 물을 주었다	the seeds 씨앗들에	every day. 매일

5 며칠 후, 씨앗이 싹을 틔웠어요.

A few days later, 며칠 후에	the seeds 씨앗은	sprouted. 싹을 틔웠다

6 하지만 잎이 호박 잎처럼 보이지 않았어요.

But 하지만	the leaves 그 잎들은	didn't look like ~처럼 보이지 않았다	pumpkin leaves. 호박 잎들

7 잭은 자신의 식물을 주의 깊게 지켜봤어요.

Jack 잭은	watched 지켜봤다	his plant 그의 식물을	carefully. 주의 깊게

8 그리고 오이가 자라기 시작했어요!

Then, 그리고	a cucumber 오이가	started 시작했다	to grow! 자라는 것을

9 식물들을 보여주는 시간이 되었어요.

It was time 때가 되었다	to show 보여줄	the plants. 식물들을

10 모두 자신의 호박을 가져왔어요.

Everyone 모두가	brought 가져왔다	their pumpkins. 그들의 호박을

Unit 8 Saving Sea Animals

READ AND WRITE 문장을 의미 단위로 나눠 읽은 뒤, 전체 문장을 따라 쓰세요.

1 바다에 쓰레기가 너무 많아요.

There is	too much trash	in the sea.
~가 있다	너무 많은 쓰레기	바다에

2 우리 바다 동물 구조 센터는 다친 동물들을 도와요.

Our Sea Animal Rescue Center	helps	the hurt animals.
우리의 바다 동물 구조 센터는	돕는다	다친 동물들을

3 비닐봉지가 펭귄의 머리에 꽉 끼어 있었어요.

A plastic bag	was stuck	on a penguin's head.
비닐봉지가	꽉 끼어 있다	펭귄의 머리에

4 그것은 숨을 잘 쉴 수 없었어요.

It	couldn't breathe	well.
그것은 (= 펭귄은)	숨을 쉴 수 없었다	잘

5 우리는 조심히 봉지를 빼주었어요.

We	carefully	took the bag off.
우리는	조심히	봉지를 뺐다

6 뾰족한 빨대가 거북의 코에 박혀 있었어요.

A sharp straw	was stuck	in a turtle's nose.
뾰족한 빨대가	박혀 있었다	거북의 코에

7 돌고래가 기름 유출 지역을 헤엄쳤어요.

A dolphin	swam	through an oil spill.
돌고래가	헤엄쳤다	기름 유출 지역을 통과하여

8 바다표범이 낚시 그물에 엉켜 있었어요.

A seal	got tangled	in a fishing net.
바다표범이	엉켜 있었다	낚시 그물에

9 우리는 바다에 쓰레기를 버리면 안 돼요.

We	must not	throw trash	into the sea.
우리는	~해서는 안 된다	쓰레기를 버린다	바다에

10 그러면 바다 동물들이 안전하게 살 수 있어요.

Then,	sea animals	can live	safely.
그러면	바다 동물들이	살 수 있다	안전하게

GREAT JOB

3B

기적의 영어리딩

Answer Key

Unit 1

Ride Safely

안전하게 타기

Key Words

helmet 헬멧	**protect** 보호하다	**ride** (자전거 등을) 타다	**road** 도로, 길
hill 언덕	**puddle** 물웅덩이	**slippery** 미끄러운	**size** 크기

Sentence Patterns

• We have to ______.	우리는 ~해야 해요.
• I wait until ______.	나는 ~할 때까지 기다려요.
• Watch out for ______!	~을 조심해!

Story Reading

p.14

나는 자전거 타는 것을 아주 좋아해요.
안전하게 지내려면, 몇 가지 규칙을 따라야 해요.

나는 항상 헬멧을 써요.
헬멧은 내 머리를 보호해요.

p.15

나는 (차들이 다니는) 도로가 아니라 자전거 전용 도로에서 타요.
나는 사람들을 치지 않도록 조심해요.
"조심해요!"

나는 항상 빨간불에서 멈춰요.
나는 초록불로 바뀔 때까지 기다려요.

p.16

나는 언덕에서는 천천히 가요.
빠르게 가면 위험할 수 있어요!

"괜찮아?"
물웅덩이를 조심하세요!
젖은 길은 미끄러울 수 있어요.

p.17

내 남동생도 자전거를 타고 싶어 해요.
"규칙 하나 더! 너에게 맞는 크기의 자전거를 골라."

나는 그가 세발자전거에 올라타도록 도와줘요.
"이제 너한테 딱 맞는 자전거가 생겼네!"

Answers

p.13

A 단어와 우리말 뜻을 알맞게 연결하세요.

1. protect – 보호하다
2. hill – 언덕
3. size – 크기
4. slippery – 미끄러운

B 우리말 뜻에 맞는 단어가 되도록 빈칸에 알맞은 글자를 쓰세요.

1. (자전거 등을) 타다: r **i** d **e**
2. 헬멧: h **e** l **m** **e** t
3. 도로, 길: r **o** a d
4. 물웅덩이: p **u** **d** d l e

p.18 Comprehension

A 보기에서 알맞은 단어를 골라 빈칸에 쓰세요.

slippery lane ride helmet hill

1. My little brother wants to **ride**, too.
2. Wet roads can be **slippery**.
3. I always wear a **helmet**.
4. I go slow on **hill**s.
5. I ride in the bike **lane**, not on the road.

p.19

B 그림을 보고 알맞은 문장에 ✓ 표시를 하세요.

1. ✓ Watch out for puddles! / Watch out for people!
2. I help him onto his tricycle. / ✓ I ride in the bike lane, not on the road.
3. ✓ I always stop at a red light. / I always stop at a green light.

C 다음 문장이 옳으면 T(True), 틀리면 F(False)에 동그라미 하세요.

1. This story is about how to ride a bike fast. — **F**
2. A helmet protects his arms. — **F**
3. The boy rides his bike carefully. — **T**

p.20

D 빈칸에 알맞은 단어를 넣어 자전거 안전 규칙을 완성하세요.

You should ...

- always wear a **helmet**.
- **stop** at a red light.
- go **slow** on hills.
- watch out for puddles.
- choose the right **size** bike for you.

slow stop helmet size

Think & Say

신호등이 빨간 불로 바뀌면 어떻게 해야 할까요?

- Cross before any cars come. (차들이 오기 전에 건너요.)
- ✓ Stop and get off my bike. (멈추고 자전거에서 내려요.)
- Ring the bell and cross the street. (벨을 울리고 길을 건너요.)

*cross 건너다

p.21 Listen Again

스토리를 다시 들으며 빈칸에 알맞은 단어를 써 넣으세요.

I love riding my **bike**. To stay safe, we have to follow some rules.

I always wear a **helmet**. It **protect**s my head.

I ride in the **bike lane**, not on the road. I am careful not to hit people. I always stop at a red light. I wait until it turns green.

I go slow on **hill**s. Going fast can be dangerous! Watch out for **puddle**s! Wet roads can be **slippery**.

My little brother wants to **ride**, too. "One more rule! Choose the right **size** bike for you." I help him onto his **tricycle**. "Now you have the perfect bike!"

helmet, protect, puddle, bike lane, hill, tricycle, size, bike, slippery, ride

p.22 Sentence Patterns

다음 필수 문형을 다양한 예문에 적용해 보세요.

1 We have to ____ . 우리는 ~해야 해요.

1. 우리는 몇 가지 규칙들을 따라야 해요. We have to **follow some rules**.
2. 우리는 우리의 친구를 도와야 해요. We have to **help our friends**.
3. 우리는 플라스틱을 재활용해야 해요. We have to **recycle plastic**.

2 I wait until ____ . 나는 ~할 때까지 기다려요.

1. 나는 초록불로 바뀔 때까지 기다려요. I wait until **it turns green**.
2. 나는 비가 멈출 때까지 기다려요. I wait until **the rain stops**.
3. 나는 페인트가 마를 때까지 기다려요. I wait until **the paint dries**.

Word Box: recycle plastic, the paint dries, bees, help our friends, the rain stops, rocks

p.23

3 Watch out for ____ ! ~을 조심해!

1. 물웅덩이를 조심해! Watch out for **puddles**!
2. 바위들을 조심해! Watch out for **rocks**!
3. 벌들을 조심해! Watch out for **bees**!

Try Writing 배운 필수 문형을 활용해 영작해 보세요.

1. 깨진 유리를 조심해! (the broken glass) **Watch out for the broken glass!**
2. 우리는 손을 씻어야 해요. (wash our hands) **We have to wash our hands.**
3. 나는 물이 끓을 때까지 기다려요. (the water boils) **I wait until the water boils.**

p.24 Think More

Ride Safely!

★ 알맞은 단어를 골라 자전거를 안전하게 타는 방법을 완성하세요.

- Wear a (**helmet** / hat).
- Wear (dark / **bright**) clothes.
- Use the (road / **bike lane**).
- Stop at a (green / **red**) light.
- Look (one / **both**) ways before crossing.
- Don't go too (**fast** / slow) on hills.

*dark 어두운 bright 밝은

안전하게 타요!

- 헬멧을 쓰세요.
- 밝은 옷을 입으세요.
- 자전거 전용 도로를 이용하세요.
- 빨간불에서는 멈추세요.
- 길을 건너기 전에 양쪽을 살펴보세요.
- 언덕에서는 너무 빨리 가지 마세요.

Unit 2

My Summer Vacation

나의 여름 방학

Key Words

vacation 방학	**late** 늦게	**schedule** 일정, 스케줄	**write** 쓰다, 적다
wake up (잠에서) 깨다, 일어나다	**bored** 지루해하는	**laugh** 웃다	**jump rope** 줄넘기를 하다

Sentence Patterns

• **How about ______ -ing ?**	~하는 게 어때?
• **It looks ______ to me.**	그것은 나에게 ~해 보여요.
• **I tried to ______ .**	나는 ~하려고 노력했어요.

Story Reading

p.28

여름 방학이 오늘 시작됐어요.
나는 게을러서 늦게 일어났어요.
나는 하루 종일 친구들과 놀았어요.
"하루 계획표를 만드는 건 어때?"
엄마가 말해요.

p.29

나는 앉아서 하루 계획표를 써요.
"7시에 일어난다. 12시에 점심 먹는다. 2시에 책을 읽는다."
엄마가 말해요. "정말 훌륭한 계획이구나!"
하지만 내게는 지루해 보여요.

p.30

다음 날, 나는 내 계획표를 지키려고 노력했어요.
나는 7시에 일어났지만 다시 잠들었어요.

나는 2시에 책을 폈지만 지루해졌어요.
나는 재미로 컴퓨터 게임을 하기 시작했어요.

내가 지루함을 느낄 때는 bored, 어떤 대상이 지루할 때는 boring을 써요.
I'm bored. 나는 지루해.
It's boring. 그건 지루해.

p.31

"오, 안 돼. 오늘은 계획대로 되지 않았어."
엄마가 웃어요.
"자기 전에 아직 줄넘기를 할 수 있잖아!"

"야호, 오늘 계획 중에 한 가지는 했어!"

Answers

p.27

A

1 wake up — 방학
2 jump rope — 줄넘기를 하다
3 schedule — (잠에서) 깨다, 일어나다
4 vacation — 일정, 스케줄

B

b	i	u	r	e	z	o	w
y	s	d	m	j	x	c	r
k	b	o	r	e	d	a	i
t	j	q	o	i	o	y	t
n	f	l	e	b	v	q	e
w	j	a	t	r	c	m	h
c	k	t	l	a	u	g	h
g	u	e	i	n	d	s	f

1 늦게 late
2 웃다 laugh
3 지루해하는 bored
4 쓰다, 적다 write

p.32 Comprehension

A wake up / jump rope / vacation / schedule / bored

1 I opened a book at 2, but I got bored.
2 "You can still jump rope before bed!"
3 Summer vacation began today.
4 "Wake up at 7. Eat lunch at 12. Read at 2."
5 "How about making a daily schedule?"

p.33

B
1 V I was lazy, and I got up late.
I was lazy, and I opened a book.
2 V I played with my friends all day.
I jumped rope all day.
3 I started reading a book for fun.
V I started playing computer games for fun.

C
1 The boy jumped rope before bed. (T)
2 The boy said, "It's a great plan!" (F)
3 The boy woke up late on the first day. (T)

p.34

D

My Daily Schedule (계획)	What I Really Did (내가 실제로 한 일)
Wake up at 7.	ⓒ
ⓑ	I opened a book, but I got bored.
Jump rope at 7.	ⓐ

ⓐ I did it!
ⓑ Read at 2.
ⓒ I woke up at 7, but I fell asleep again.

Think & Say
Jump rope is good for your health.
V It's good to make a plan.
You should read books every day.

p.35 Listen Again

Summer vacation began today. I was lazy, and I got up late. I played with my friends all day. "How about making a daily schedule?" Mom says.

I sit and write my daily schedule. "Wake up at 7. Eat lunch at 12. Read at 2." Mom says, "It's a great plan!" But it looks boring to me.

The next day, I tried to follow my schedule. I woke up at 7, but I fell asleep again. I opened a book at 2, but I got bored. I started playing computer games for fun.

"Oh no, today didn't go as planned." Mom laughs. "You can still jump rope before bed!"

"Yay! I did one thing on my schedule today!"

p.36 Sentence Patterns

1 How about ___-ing?
How about making a daily schedule?
How about planting a tree?
How about watching a movie?

2 It looks ___ to me.
It looks boring to me.
It looks fun to me.
It looks scary to me.

p.37

3 I tried to ___.
I tried to follow my schedule.
I tried to catch the butterfly.
I tried to finish my homework.

Try Writing
1 How about reading a book?
2 It looks interesting to me.
3 I tried to solve the puzzle.

p.38 My Daily Schedule

1. What time do you get up? — I get up at 7 a.m.
2. When do you read books? — I read books at 2 p.m.
3. What do you do from 9 to 11 a.m.? — practice the piano
4. What do you do after dinner? — jump rope after dinner.

나의 하루 계획표

1. 너는 몇 시에 일어나니? – 아침 7시에 일어나요.
2. 너는 언제 책을 읽니? – 오후 2시에 책을 읽어요.
3. 너는 오전 9시부터 11시까지 무엇을 하니? – 피아노를 연습해요.
4. 너는 저녁 식사 후에 무엇을 하니? – 저녁 식사 후에 줄넘기를 해요.

Unit 3

The Rainy Barbecue

비 오는 날의 바비큐 파티

Key Words

set up 준비하다	**light** 불을 붙이다	**dark** 검은, 어두운	**yesterday** 어제
forecast 예보	**pour** (비가) 마구 쏟아지다	**sandwich** 샌드위치	**picnic** 소풍

Sentence Patterns

• **It'll be ______ all day.**	하루 종일 (날씨가) ~할 거예요.
• **______ went out.**	~가 꺼졌어요.
• **It's fun to ______.**	~하는 것은 재미있어요.

Story Reading

p.42

알렉스의 가족은 오늘 바비큐 파티를 해요.
"하루 종일 맑을 거야." 아빠가 말했어요.

그들은 그릴을 설치했어요.
아빠는 바비큐를 하려고 불을 붙였어요.

p.43

갑자기 강한 바람이 불었어요.
불이 꺼지고, 엄마의 스카프가 날아가 버렸어요!
"내 스카프!" 엄마는 그것을 따라 달렸어요.
"오늘은 정말 맑지 않아요!"

p.44

검은 구름이 하늘에 나타났어요.
곧 비가 내리기 시작했어요.
"전혀 맑지 않은데요." 알렉스가 말했어요.
모두 비를 피하려고 달렸어요.

아빠가 휴대전화를 확인했어요.
"이런! 내가 어제 일기 예보를 봤어!"

cover: (좋지 않은 날씨 등을) 피할 곳, 몸을 숨길 곳

p.45

비가 쏟아지고, 바람이 더 거세졌어요.
텐트가 날아가 버렸어요.
엄마는 샌드위치를 꺼냈어요.
"비 오는 날에 소풍을 하는 것도 재미있네." 엄마가 말했어요.

Answers

p.41

A
1 sandwich — 샌드위치
2 yesterday — 어제
3 picnic — 소풍
4 set up — 준비하다

B
1 dark
2 light
3 forecast
4 pour

p.46 Comprehension

A dark / forecast / set up / sandwich / pour

1 It **pour**ed, and the wind grew stronger.
2 **Dark** clouds appeared in the sky.
3 They **set up** the grill.
4 Mom took out our **sandwich**es.
5 "Oh no! I looked at yesterday's **forecast**!"

p.47

B
1 V Dad lit the fire for the barbecue. / Dad checked his phone.
2 V It'll be sunny all day. / It's not sunny at all.
3 V They ran for cover. / They took out their sandwiches.

C
1 Dad said it would be sunny all day. — T
2 A strong wind blew Mom's hat away. — F
3 Dad checked yesterday's forecast by mistake. — T

p.48

D
ⓐ Mom's scarf flew away!
ⓑ Dark clouds appeared, and it started to rain.
ⓒ Mom said, "It's fun to have a picnic in the rain."
ⓓ Dad said, "It'll be sunny all day!"

ⓓ → ⓐ → ⓑ → ⓒ

Think & Say
grill the food / play games / go fishing / eat together
I like to ____ when I go camping with my family.

나는 가족과 캠핑을 갈 때 ________하는 것을 좋아해.

p.49 Listen Again

Alex's family is having a **barbecue** today. "It'll be sunny all day," Dad said. They **set up** the grill. Dad **lit** the fire for the barbecue.

Suddenly, a strong **wind** blew. The fire went out, and Mom's scarf flew away! "My scarf!" Mom ran after it. "It's not really **sunny** today!"

Dark clouds **appear**ed in the sky. Soon, it started to rain. "It's not sunny at all," Alex said. Everyone ran for cover.
Dad checked his phone. "Oh no! I looked at yesterday's **forecast**!"

It **pour**ed, and the wind grew stronger. The tent blew away. Mom took out our **sandwich**es. "It's fun to have a **picnic** in the rain," Mom said.

pour / lit / sandwich / picnic / barbecue / sunny / appear / set up / forecast / wind

p.50 Sentence Patterns

1 It'll be ____ all day.
It'll be **sunny** all day.
It'll be **rainy** all day.
It'll be **snowy** all day.

2 ____ went out.
The fire went out.
The light went out.
The candle went out.

p.51

3 It's fun to ____.
It's fun to **have a picnic**.
It's fun to **kick a ball**.
It's fun to **open a gift**.

Try Writing
1 **It'll be windy all day.**
2 **The flashlight went out.**
3 **It's fun to take pictures.**

p.52 Think More

The Weather Forecast

Monday	Tuesday	Wednesday	Thursday
18°	15°	18°	17°

Friday	Saturday	Sunday
-1°	13°	10°

How many days will be sunny? — There will be **three** sunny days.
Which day will be cloudy? — It will be cloudy on **Tuesday**.
Which day will be rainy? — It will be rainy on **Sunday**.
Which day will be the coldest? — The coldest day will be **Friday**.

일기 예보

- 며칠이나 맑을까요? – 맑은 날은 사흘일 거예요.
- 어느 날이 흐릴까요? – 화요일에 흐릴 거예요.
- 어느 날이 비가 올까요? – 일요일에 비가 올 거예요.
- 어느 날이 가장 추울까요? – 가장 추운 날은 금요일이에요.

Unit 4

The Flying Helpers

하늘을 나는 도움 요원

Key Words

drone 드론	**farmer** 농부	**field** 들판, 밭	**check** 점검하다, 살피다
crop 농작물	**crack** (갈라져 생긴) 금	**wild** 야생의	**traffic** 차량들, 교통

Sentence Patterns

• **It can help ________.**	그것은 ~을 도울 수 있어요.
• **It checks if ________.**	그것은 ~인지 아닌지를 점검해요.
• **Maybe we will have ________.**	아마도 우리는 ~을 가지게 될 거예요.

Story Reading

p.56

따르릉! 드론 센터에는 전화가 많이 와요.
사람들은 하늘을 나는 도움 요원들이 필요해요.
드론들이 도울 준비가 되어 있어요!

p.57

드론은 농부를 도울 수 있어요.
드론이 들판 위를 날아요.
농작물이 건강한지를 점검해요.

드론은 소방관을 도울 수 있어요.
위험에 처한 사람들을 찾을 수 있어요.

p.58

드론은 기술자를 도울 수 있어요.
높은 건물들을 점검해요.
금이 간 곳이나 다른 문제들을 찾아요.

드론은 과학자를 도울 수 있어요.
야생동물을 놀라게 하지 않고 지켜봐요.

p.59

아마도 가까운 미래에는 드론 택시가 생길 거예요.
도로 위를 날 수도 있겠죠.
더 이상 교통 체증은 없어요!
정말 고마워요, 드론 센터!

Answers

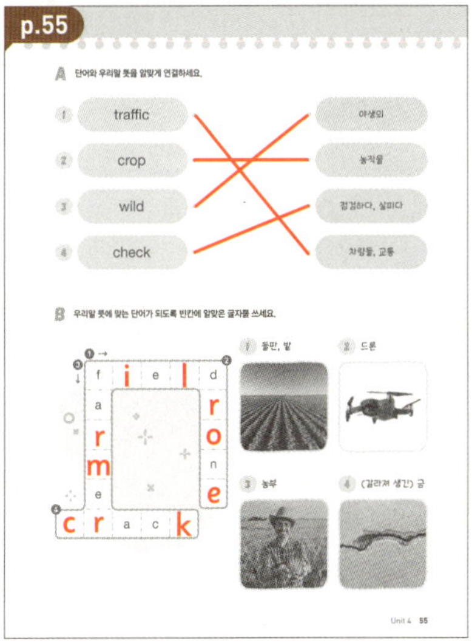
p.55

A 단어와 우리말 뜻을 알맞게 연결하세요.

1 traffic — 차량들, 교통
2 crop — 농작물
3 wild — 야생의
4 check — 점검하다, 살피다

B 우리말 뜻에 맞는 단어가 되도록 빈칸에 알맞은 글자를 쓰세요.

1 들판, 밭 — field
2 드론 — drone
3 농부 — farmer
4 (갈라져 생긴) 금 — crack

p.60 Comprehension

A 보기에서 알맞은 단어를 골라 빈칸에 쓰세요.

firefighter animal field crack taxi

1 A drone can help firefighters.
2 A drone looks for cracks or other problems.
3 A drone flies over a field.
4 Maybe we will have drone taxis in the near future.
5 A drone watches wild animals without scaring them.

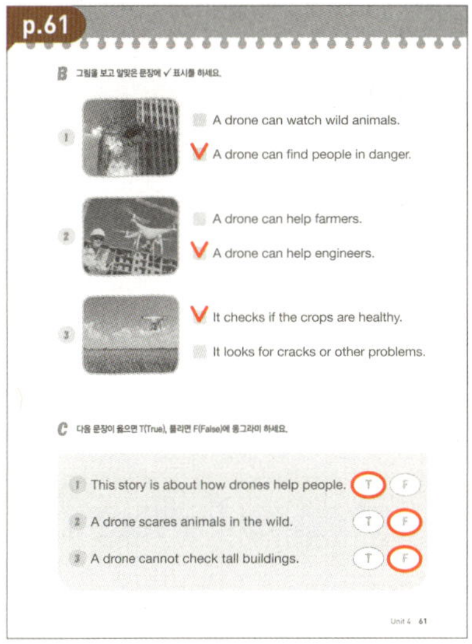
p.61

B 그림을 보고 알맞은 문장에 ✓ 표시를 하세요.

1 A drone can watch wild animals. / ✓ A drone can find people in danger.
2 A drone can help farmers. / ✓ A drone can help engineers.
3 ✓ It checks if the crops are healthy. / It looks for cracks or other problems.

C 다음 문장이 옳으면 T(True), 틀리면 F(False)에 동그라미 하세요.

1 This story is about how drones help people. (T)
2 A drone scares animals in the wild. (F)
3 A drone cannot check tall buildings. (F)

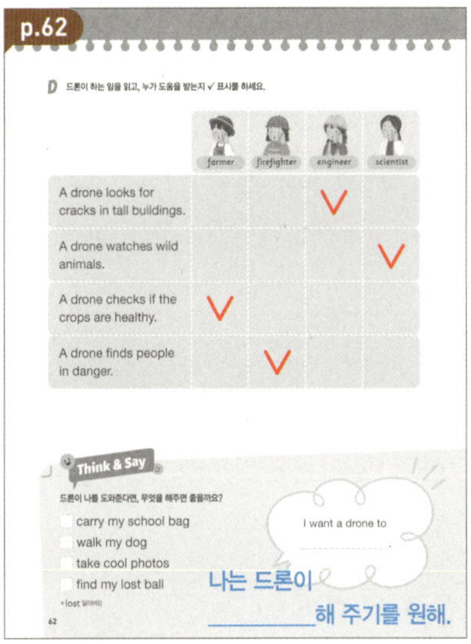
p.62

D 드론이 하는 일을 읽고, 누가 도움을 받는지 ✓ 표시를 하세요.

	farmer	firefighter	engineer	scientist
A drone looks for cracks in tall buildings.			✓	
A drone watches wild animals.				✓
A drone checks if the crops are healthy.	✓			
A drone finds people in danger.		✓		

Think & Say

드론이 나를 도와준다면, 무엇을 해주면 좋을까요?

carry my school bag
walk my dog
take cool photos
find my lost ball

I want a drone to ______.

나는 드론이 ______ 해 주기를 원해.

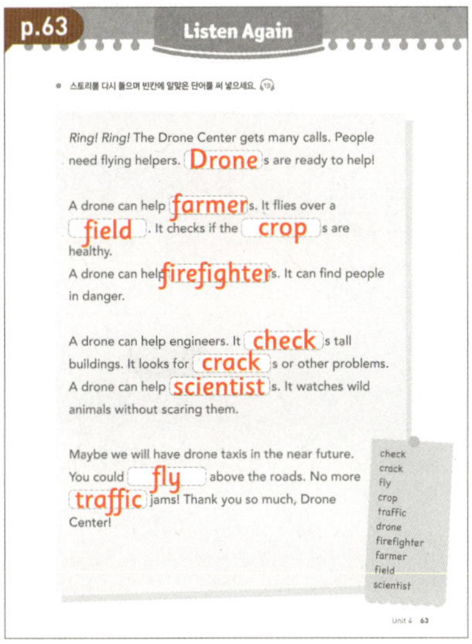
p.63 Listen Again

스토리를 다시 들으며 빈칸에 알맞은 단어를 써 넣으세요.

Ring! Ring! The Drone Center gets many calls. People need flying helpers. Drones are ready to help!

A drone can help farmers. It flies over a field. It checks if the crops are healthy.
A drone can help firefighters. It can find people in danger.

A drone can help engineers. It checks tall buildings. It looks for cracks or other problems.
A drone can help scientists. It watches wild animals without scaring them.

Maybe we will have drone taxis in the near future. You could fly above the roads. No more traffic jams! Thank you so much, Drone Center!

check crack fly crop traffic drone firefighter farmer field scientist

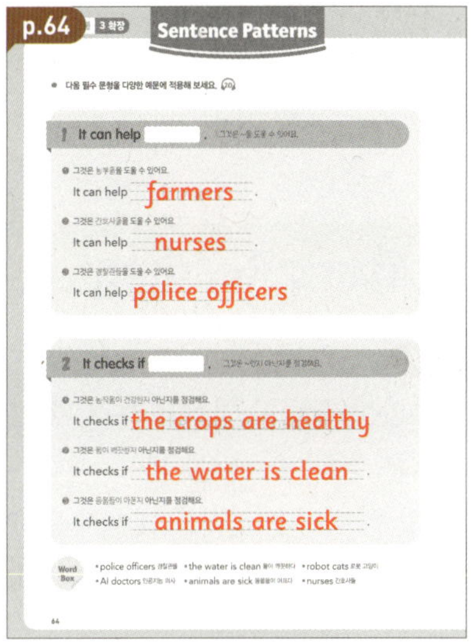
p.64 Sentence Patterns

1 It can help ______. 그것은 ~을 도울 수 있어요.
It can help farmers.
It can help nurses.
It can help police officers.

2 It checks if ______. 그것은 ~인지 아닌지를 점검해요.
It checks if the crops are healthy.
It checks if the water is clean.
It checks if animals are sick.

Word Box: police officers, the water is clean, robot cats, AI doctors, animals are sick, nurses

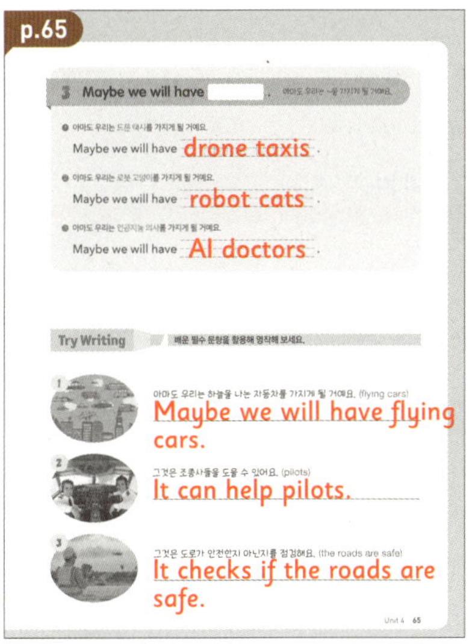
p.65

3 Maybe we will have ______. 아마도 우리는 ~을 가지게 될 거예요.
Maybe we will have drone taxis.
Maybe we will have robot cats.
Maybe we will have AI doctors.

Try Writing 배운 필수 문형을 활용해 영작해 보세요.

1 아마도 우리는 하늘을 나는 자동차를 가지게 될 거예요. (flying cars)
Maybe we will have flying cars.
2 그것은 조종사들을 도울 수 있어요. (pilots)
It can help pilots.
3 그것은 도로가 안전한지 아닌지를 점검해요. (the roads are safe)
It checks if the roads are safe.

p.66 Think More

What Can Drones Do?

Drones can carry small things.
Drones can water plants.
Drones can make beautiful fireworks.
Drones can find lost people.
Drones can film movies.

make water find carry

드론은 무엇을 할 수 있을까요?

- 드론은 작은 물건을 나를 수 있어요.
- 드론은 식물에 물을 줄 수 있어요.
- 드론은 아름다운 불꽃놀이를 만들 수 있어요.
- 드론은 길을 잃은 사람들을 찾을 수 있어요.
- 드론은 영화를 촬영할 수 있어요.

Unit 5

Pick a Movie!

영화를 골라봐!

Key Words

movie 영화	superhero 슈퍼히어로	brave 용감한	fight 싸우다
finger 손가락	wizard 마법사	choose 선택하다, 고르다	decide 결정하다

Sentence Patterns

• They talk about ________.	그들은 ~에 대해 이야기해요.
• There are ________.	~들이 있어요.
• It's hard to ________.	~하기 어려워요.

Story Reading

p.74

엄마와 친구들이 영화를 보러 가요.
그들은 영화 포스터를 봐요.
"정말 선택지가 많아!" 엄마가 말해요.
그들은 어떤 영화를 볼지 이야기해요.

p.75

잭은 슈퍼히어로 영화를 보고 싶어해요.
"슈퍼히어로는 용감하고 힘이 세.
그들은 악당들과 싸우고 사람들을 도와줘."

그는 슈퍼히어로처럼 손을 뻗어요.

p.76

판타지 영화는 소피아의 선택이에요.
"하늘을 나는 책과 말하는 모자가 있어.
이 이야기는 놀라움으로 가득할 거야!"

"아브라카다브라!" (= 수리수리 마수리!)

소피아는 마법사처럼 손가락을 흔들어요.

p.77

엠마는 동물 영화를 골라요.
"동물들이 함께 여행을 가.
재미있어 보이네." 그녀가 말해요.

"결정하기 어려워.
먼저 팝콘부터 사자!" 잭이 말해요.

Answers

p.73

A 단어와 우리말 뜻을 알맞게 연결하세요.

1 choose — 선택하다, 고르다
2 wizard — 마법사
3 superhero — 슈퍼히어로
4 finger — 손가락

B 다음 우리말 뜻에 맞는 단어를 찾아 동그라미 하고 한 번 쓰세요.

h	y	d	t	m	a	d	i
o	j	s	g	p	r	e	v
b	r	a	v	e	u	c	k
r	f	n	w	q	l	i	z
c	l	p	a	b	t	d	d
y	g	u	h	j	g	e	s
l	h	t	m	o	v	i	e
u	t	e	k	b	x	n	f

1 용감한 brave
2 영화 movie
3 싸우다 fight
4 결정하다 decide

p.78 Comprehension

A 보기에서 알맞은 단어를 골라 빈칸에 쓰세요.

movie decide fight superhero animal

1 "It's hard to **decide**. Let's get some popcorn first!"
2 Emma chooses the **animal** movie.
3 He holds out his hand like a **superhero**.
4 "They **fight** bad guys and help people."
5 They talk about which **movie** to see.

p.79

B 그림을 보고 알맞은 문장에 ✓ 표시를 하세요.

1 Sophia fights bad guys. / ✓ Sophia waves her finger like a wizard.
2 They look at the books. / ✓ They look at the movie posters.
3 ✓ The animals go on a trip together. / The animals help people.

C 다음 문장이 옳으면 T(True), 틀리면 F(False)에 동그라미 하세요.

1 Emma and her friends go on a trip. T **F**
2 They talk about which game to play. T **F**
3 There are talking hats in the superhero movie. T **F**

p.80

D 빈칸에 알맞은 단어를 써서 영화 소개를 완성하세요.

the animal movie
· animals going on a **trip**
· an **exciting** story

the superhero movie
· brave and **strong** superheroes
· fighting bad guys and helping people

the fantasy movie
· **flying** books and talking hats
· a story full of **surprise**s

strong flying surprise trip exciting

Think & Say

아주 재미있게 본 영화는 어떤 종류의 영화인가요?

- a comedy movie
- a fantasy movie
- an action movie
- an animated movie

I like ____ (종류). 나는 ____을 좋아해.
My favorite movie is ____ (제목). 내가 가장 좋아하는 영화는 ____야.

p.81 Listen Again

스토리를 다시 들으며 빈칸에 알맞은 단어를 써 넣으세요.

Emma and her friends go to the movies. They look at the movie **poster**s. "So many choices!" Emma says. They talk about which **movie** to see.

Jack wants to see the superhero movie. "Superheroes are **brave** and strong. They fight bad guys and help people." He holds out his hand like a **superhero**.

The **fantasy** movie is Sophia's pick. "There are flying books and talking hats. The story will be full of **surprise**s!" Sophia waves her finger like a **wizard**.

Emma **choose**s the animal movie. "The animals go on a **trip** together. It looks exciting," she says. "It's hard to **decide**. Let's get some popcorn first!" Jack says.

wizard brave choose poster trip surprise superhero decide movie fantasy

p.82 Sentence Patterns

다음 필수 문형을 다양한 예문에 적용해 보세요.

1 They talk about ____. 그들은 ~에 대해 이야기해요.

- They talk about **which movie to see**.
- They talk about **which game to play**.
- They talk about **which bus to take**.

2 There are ____. ~들이 있어요.

- There are **flying books**.
- There are **talking parrots**.
- There are **singing cats**.

Word Box: which game to play · which bus to take · talking parrots · singing cats · remember · wait

p.83

3 It's hard to ____. ~하기 어려워요.

- 결정하기 어려워요. It's hard to **decide**.
- 기다리기 어려워요. It's hard to **wait**.
- 기억하기 어려워요. It's hard to **remember**.

Try Writing 배운 필수 문형을 활용해 영작해 보세요.

1 펄럭이는 깃발들이 있어요. (waving flags) **There are waving flags.**
2 그들은 어느 셔츠를 입을지에 대해 이야기해요. (which shirt to wear) **They talk about which shirt to wear.**
3 웃기 어려워요. (smile) **It's hard to smile.**

p.84 Think More

At the Movies

NOW SHOWING	
Space Journey	9:00
Superhero Power	9:30
Animal Friends	10:00
A Day in the Park	10:30
The Wizard's Dragon	11:00

It's a movie with a brave and strong superhero. It will be exciting. It starts at 9:30. — **Superhero Power**

I choose the fantasy movie. A dragon and a wizard will have an adventure. It starts at 11:00. — **The Wizard's Dragon**

영화관에서

지금 상영 중이에요!
우주 여행
슈퍼히어로 파워
동물 친구들
공원에서의 하루
마법사의 드래곤

• 용감하고 힘센 슈퍼히어로가 나오는 영화예요. 재미있을 거예요. 9시 30분에 시작해요.

• 나는 판타지 영화를 선택할래요. 드래곤과 마법사가 모험을 할 거예요. 11시에 시작해요.

Unit 6

The Lost Kitten

길을 잃은 아기 고양이

Key Words

find (우연히) 찾다, 발견하다	**kitten** 새끼 고양이	**hide** 숨다	**gray** 회색의, 회색
lost 잃어버린, 길을 잃은	**string** 끈	**poster** 포스터, 벽보	**call** 전화하다

Sentence Patterns

• I found ______ in ______.	나는 ~을 …에서 찾았어요.
• I named ______ ______.	나는 ~을 …라고 이름 지었어요.
• I was sad to ______.	나는 ~해서 슬펐어요.

Story Reading

p.88

4월 1일

오늘 나는 뒷마당에서 아기 고양이를 발견했다.
그 고양이는 덤불 속에 숨어 있었다.
작고 회색이었다.
엄마가 말했다. "우리가 길을 잃은 아기 고양이를 도와주자."

p.89

4월 3일

나는 아기 고양이에게 '마일로'라고 이름을 지었다.
마일로는 줄 가지고 노는 걸 좋아한다.
우리는 포스터를 만들었다. "당신의 고양이인가요?"
우리는 그 포스터를 공원에 붙였다.

당신의 고양이인가요?

- 작고 회색임
- 상냥하고 온순함
- 4월 1일에 발견됨

전화주세요.

p.90

4월 7일

어느 여자분이 마일로에 대해 전화를 했다.
그분이 말했다. "그건 제 고양이에요!"
그분은 와서 마일로를 집으로 데려갔다.
나는 작별 인사를 해서 슬펐지만, 마일로가 가족을 찾아서 기뻤다.

p.91

4월 10일

나는 마일로의 집에 방문했다.
그는 내 무릎에 앉아서 가르랑거렸다.
그 여자분이 말했다. "얘를 구해줘서 고마워요."
"그가 집에 돌아가서 정말 기뻐요." 나는 웃었다.

Answers

p.87

A

1. string — 끈
2. call — 전화하다
3. kitten — 새끼 고양이
4. lost — 잃어버린, 길을 잃은

B

1 poster (p o s t e r) — 포스터, 벽보
2 gray (g r a y) — 회색의, 회색
3 find (f i n d) — (우연히) 찾다, 발견하다
4 hide (h i d e) — 숨다

p.92 Comprehension

A gray / family / poster / visit / string

1. We made a **poster**: "Is This Your Cat?"
2. It was small and **gray**.
3. I **visit**ed Milo at his house.
4. Milo likes to play with **string**.
5. I was sad to say good-bye but happy Milo found his **family**.

p.93

B

1. ✓ The kitten likes to play with string.
2. ✓ I found a kitten in my backyard.
3. ✓ The kitten sat on my lap.

C

1. The kitten was hiding in a bush. — T
2. Mom named the kitten Milo. — F
3. They put up the poster at the park. — T

p.94

D

I found a **kitten** in my backyard. I named the kitten **Milo**.

We **made** a poster: "Is This Your Cat?"

A lady said, "That's my kitten!" She came and took Milo **home**.

I visited Milo at his house. He sat on my **lap** and purred.

lap / Milo / kitten / made / home

Think & Say

1. The girl finds a lost kitten. — ✓ worried
2. The kitten goes back to the lady. — ✓ sad
3. The girl visits the kitten and sees he is safe. — ✓ happy

p.95 Listen Again

[April 1] Today, I found a kitten in my **backyard**. It was hiding in a bush. It was small and **gray**. Mom said, "Let's help the **lost** kitten."

[April 3] I **name**d the kitten Milo. Milo likes to play with **string**. We made a **poster**: "Is This Your Cat?" We put it up at the park.

[April 7] A lady called about Milo. She said, "That's my **kitten**!" She came and took Milo home. I was sad to say good-bye but happy Milo found his **family**.

[April 10] I **visit**ed Milo at his house. He sat on my lap and **purr**ed. The lady said, "Thank you for saving him." "I'm so glad he is back home," I smiled.

p.96 Sentence Patterns

1 I found ___ in ___.

- I found **a kitten** in **my backyard**.
- I found **a frog** in **the pond**.
- I found **a snail** in **the garden**.

2 I named ___ ___.

- I named **the kitten Milo**.
- I named **the dog Max**.
- I named **the fish Goldie**.

p.97

3 I was sad to ___.

- I was sad to **say good-bye**.
- I was sad to **lose the game**.
- I was sad to **leave my friend**.

Try Writing

1. I found a ball in the park.
2. I named the turtle Speedy.
3. I was sad to hear the news.

p.98 Think More

Found Cat

Is This Your Cat?

I found this cat near Maple Park on August 15.
It has short brown fur.
It has black stripes on its legs.

Please call Stella: 010-111-1234

(✓ 2번째 고양이)

고양이를 찾았어요

당신의 고양이인가요?

8월 15일 메이플 공원 근처에서 이 고양이를 발견했어요.
짧은 갈색 털을 가졌어요.
다리에는 검은 줄무늬가 있어요.

스텔라에게 전화해 주세요.

Unit 7 The Pumpkin Growing Contest

호박 키우기 대회

Key Words

pumpkin 호박	**seed** 씨	**plant** (씨앗 등을) 심다, 식물	**grow** 기르다, 자라다
sprout 싹이 나다, 새싹	**leaf** 잎	**cucumber** 오이	**show** 보여주다

Sentence Patterns

• I can't wait to ______ !	~하는 게 너무 기다려져요!
• ______ started to ______ .	~가 …하기 시작했어요.
• It was time to ______ .	~할 시간이었어요.

Story Reading

p.102

잭의 반에서 호박 키우기 대회를 열었어요.
그의 반 친구들 모두 호박씨를 심었어요.
잭은 말했어요. "나는 큰 호박을 키우는 게 너무 기다려져요!"

p.103

그는 매일 씨앗에 물을 주었어요.
며칠 후, 씨앗이 싹을 틔웠어요.
잭의 싹은 빠르게 자랐어요.

하지만 잎이 호박 잎처럼 보이지 않았어요.

p.104

잭은 자신의 식물을 주의 깊게 지켜보았어요.
어느 날, 작은 꽃들이 피었어요.
그리고 오이가 자라기 시작했어요!

p.105

식물을 보여주는 시간이 되었어요.
모두 자신의 호박을 가져왔어요.
"이게 내가 키운 거예요!" 잭이 말했어요.
반 친구들은 웃으며 박수를 쳤어요.
"지금까지 본 오이 중에 최고야!" 그린 선생님이 말했어요.

Answers

p.101

A

1. sprout — 싹이 나다, 새싹
2. grow — 기르다, 자라다
3. pumpkin — 호박
4. seed — 씨

B

g	s	h	o	w	e	s	b
p	j	o	r	t	l	y	n
l	u	k	z	h	e	m	i
a	f	m	d	u	a	c	g
n	r	p	i	a	f	w	k
t	x	s	g	y	o	t	q
c	u	c	u	m	b	e	r
h	d	v	l	w	j	r	f

1. 오이 cucumber
2. 잎 leaf
3. (씨앗 등을) 심다, 식물 plant
4. 보여주다 show

p.106 Comprehension

A pumpkin sprout grow cucumber flower

1. One day, small flowers came out.
2. "That's the best cucumber ever!" Ms. Green said.
3. A few days later, the seeds sprouted.
4. But the leaves didn't look like pumpkin leaves.
5. "I can't wait to grow a big pumpkin!"

p.107

B

1. ✓ Everyone planted pumpkin seeds. / Everyone watered the flowers.
2. A pumpkin started to grow! / ✓ A cucumber started to grow!
3. Everyone brought their pumpkins. / ✓ The class laughed and clapped.

C

1. Jack's class had a cucumber growing contest. — F
2. Jack watered his seeds every day. — T
3. Jack showed his pumpkin to the class. — F

p.108

D ⓓ → ⓐ → ⓑ → ⓒ

ⓐ Jack's sprout grew fast.
ⓑ The leaves didn't look like pumpkin leaves.
ⓒ Jack showed his cucumber to the class.
ⓓ Everyone in Jack's class planted pumpkin seeds.

Think & Say

✓ Give it water.
Put it in a dark place.
✓ Use good soil.
✓ Give it sunlight.

p.109 Listen Again

Jack's class had a pumpkin growing contest. Everyone in his class planted pumpkin seeds. Jack said, "I can't wait to grow a big pumpkin!"

He watered the seeds every day. A few days later, the seeds sprouted. Jack's sprout grew fast. But the leaves didn't look like pumpkin leaves.

Jack watched his plant carefully. One day, small flowers came out. Then, a cucumber started to grow!

It was time to show the plants. Everyone brought their pumpkins. "I grew this!" Jack said. The class laughed and clapped. "That's the best cucumber ever!" Ms. Green said.

clap flower show plant seed grow pumpkin sprout leaves cucumber

p.110 Sentence Patterns

1 I can't wait to ___ !

I can't wait to grow a pumpkin.
I can't wait to bake a cake!
I can't wait to make a snowman.

2 ___ started to ___ .

A cucumber started to grow.
The baby started to cry.
My ice cream started to melt.

p.111

3 It was time to ___ .

It was time to show the plants.
It was time to feed the dog.
It was time to wash the dishes.

Try Writing

1. It was time to pack my bag.
2. The leaves started to fall.
3. I can't wait to play soccer.

p.112

From Seed to Pumpkin

① A pumpkin grows from a seed.
② A seed sprouts.
③ The plant grows a long vine.
④ Yellow flowers appear.
⑤ A green pumpkin grows.
⑥ The green pumpkin turns orange.

flower orange sprout seed

씨앗에서 호박까지

1. 호박은 씨앗에서 자라요.
2. 씨앗이 싹을 틔워요.
3. 식물은 긴 덩굴을 뻗어요.
4. 노란 꽃들이 피어요.
5. 초록색 호박이 자라요.
6. 초록색 호박이 주황색으로 변해요.

Unit 8

Saving Sea Animals

바다 동물들을 지켜요

Key Words

sea 바다	**hurt** 다치게 하다, 다친	**stuck** ~에 끼어 꼼짝 못하는	**breathe** 숨을 쉬다
straw 빨대	**oil** 기름	**seal** 바다표범	**net** 그물

Sentence Patterns

• There is too much ______ in ______.	…에 ~가 너무 많아요.
• It couldn't ______.	그것은 ~할 수 없었어요.
• We must not ______.	우리는 ~하면 안 돼요.

Story Reading

p.116

바다에 쓰레기가 너무 많아요.
그것은 바다 동물들을 아프게 해요.
우리 바다 동물 구조 센터는 다친 동물들을 도와줘요.

p.117

비닐봉지가 펭귄의 머리에 꽉 끼어 있었어요.
펭귄은 숨을 잘 쉴 수 없었어요.
우리는 조심히 봉지를 빼주었어요.

뾰족한 빨대가 거북의 코에 박혀 있었어요.
우리는 그것을 살살 빼주었어요.

p.118

돌고래 한 마리가 기름 유출 지역을 헤엄쳤어요.
기름이 돌고래의 피부를 덮었어요.
우리는 돌고래를 깨끗이 씻기고 안전하게 보호했어요.

바다표범 한 마리가 낚시 그물에 엉켜 있었어요.
바다표범은 빠져나올 수 없었어요.
우리는 그물을 잘라 바다표범을 자유롭게 풀어주었어요.

p.119

우리는 바다에 쓰레기를 버리면 안 돼요.
그러면 바다 동물들이 안전하게 살 수 있어요.
우리 함께 바다를 깨끗하게 지켜요!

Answers

p.115

A 단어와 우리말 뜻을 알맞게 연결하세요.

1. stuck — ~에 끼어 꼼짝 못하는
2. net — 그물
3. oil — 기름
4. seal — 바다표범

B 우리말 뜻에 맞는 단어가 되도록 빈칸에 알맞은 글자를 쓰세요.

① 숨을 쉬다 ② 빨대 ③ 바다 ④ 다치게 하다, 다친

straw / breathe / sea / hurt

p.120 Comprehension

A 보기에서 알맞은 단어를 골라 빈칸에 쓰세요.

trash net dolphin sea breathe

1. There is too much **trash** in the sea.
2. A **dolphin** swam through an oil spill.
3. A seal got tangled in a fishing **net**.
4. A penguin couldn't **breathe** well.
5. We must not throw trash into the **sea**.

p.121

B 그림을 보고 알맞은 문장에 ✓ 표시를 하세요.

1. They throw trash into the sea. / ✓ They help keep the sea clean.
2. ✓ Too much trash hurts sea animals. / Sea animals live safely.
3. The oil covered a dolphin's skin. / ✓ The seal couldn't get out.

C 다음 문장이 옳으면 T(True), 틀리면 F(False)에 동그라미 하세요.

1. There is too much trash in the sea. — **T**
2. A turtle had a plastic bag on its head. — **F**
3. They took the hurt sea animals to the zoo. — **F**

p.122

D 위험에 빠진 동물들에게 일어난 일과 해결 방법을 정리해 보세요.

Problem(문제)	Solution(해결)
A **plastic bag** was stuck on a penguin's head.	We carefully took the bag off.
A sharp straw was stuck in a turtle's nose.	We gently took out the **straw**.
A dolphin swam through an **oil** spill.	We cleaned the dolphin and kept it safe.
A seal got tangled in a fishing net.	We cut the **net** and set the seal free.

straw oil net plastic bag

Think & Say

위험에 처한 거북이 말을 할 수 있다면, 어떤 말을 하고 싶을까요? 알맞은 말을 모두 골라 보세요.

✓ Help me. / Let's swim together. / It's sunny today. / ✓ Keep the sea clean.

p.123 Listen Again

스토리를 다시 들으며 빈칸에 알맞은 단어를 써 넣으세요.

There is too much trash in the **sea**. It hurts sea animals. Our Sea Animal Rescue Center helps the **hurt** animals.

A plastic bag was **stuck** on a penguin's head. It couldn't **breathe** well. We carefully took the bag off. A sharp **straw** was stuck in a turtle's nose. We gently took it out.

A dolphin swam through an **oil** spill. The oil covered its skin. We cleaned the dolphin and kept it safe. A **seal** got tangled in a fishing net. It couldn't get out. We cut the **net** and set it free.

We must not throw **trash** into the sea. Then, sea animals can live safely. Let's help keep the sea **clean**!

oil trash sea hurt breathe clean seal net straw stuck

p.124 Sentence Patterns

다음 필수 문형을 다양한 예문에 적용해 보세요.

1 There is too much ___ in ___.

- There is too much **trash** in **the sea**.
- There is too much **dust** in **the air**.
- There is too much **noise** in **the street**.

2 It couldn't ___.

- It couldn't **breathe well**.
- It couldn't **move fast**.
- It couldn't **jump high**.

Word Box: noise, the street / move fast / make noise / waste water / dust, the air / jump high

p.125

3 We must not ___.

- We must not **throw trash into the sea**.
- We must not **waste water**.
- We must not **make noise**.

Try Writing 배운 필수 문형을 활용해 영작해 보세요.

1. 그것은 빠르게 수영할 수 없었어요. (swim fast) — **It couldn't swim fast.**
2. 우리는 돌을 던지면 안 돼요. (throw rocks) — **We must not throw rocks.**
3. 도시에 차량이 너무 많아요. (traffic, the city) — **There is too much traffic in the city.**

p.126 Think More

Save the Ocean

- We should throw trash into the sea. — X
- We should use more plastic. — X
- We should recycle bottles and cans. — O
- We should pick up trash at the beach. — O
- We should protect sea animals in the ocean. — O
- We should try not to use plastic straws. — O

바다를 지켜요.

- 우리는 쓰레기를 바다에 버려야 해요.
- 우리는 플라스틱을 더 많이 사용해야 해요.
- 우리는 병과 캔을 재활용해야 해요.
- 우리는 해변에서 쓰레기를 주워야 해요.
- 우리는 바닷속 동물들을 보호해야 해요.
- 우리는 플라스틱 빨대를 사용하지 않도록 노력해야 해요.

Review Test 정답

p.67

Review Test 1
(Unit ① - Unit ⑥) / 25개

A 그림에 알맞은 단어를 고르세요.

1. ⓐ late **ⓑ bored** ⓒ careful
2. **ⓐ protect** ⓑ ride ⓒ laugh
3. ⓐ slippery ⓑ wild **ⓒ dark**
4. ⓐ field **ⓑ traffic** ⓒ hill
5. ⓐ set up ⓑ write **ⓒ wake up**
6. **ⓐ puddle** ⓑ crack ⓒ sandwich

Review Test 1 67

p.68

B 그림을 보고 알맞은 문장을 고르세요.

1. **ⓐ I played with my friends all day.**
   ⓑ I started playing computer games for fun.
2. **ⓐ Going fast on hills can be dangerous!**
   ⓑ Wet roads can be slippery!
3. ⓐ It'll be sunny all day.
   ⓑ It's not sunny at all.
4. **ⓐ The drone flies over a field.**
   ⓑ The drone checks tall buildings.

★★ **C** 알맞은 단어를 골라 문장을 완성하세요.

1. Alex's family (**ⓐ is** ⓑ are) having a barbecue today.
2. I love (ⓐ ride **ⓑ riding**) my bike.
3. The Drone Center gets many (ⓐ call **ⓑ calls**).
4. I was lazy, and I (ⓐ get **ⓑ got**) up late this morning.

68

p.69

D 짧은 글을 읽고 질문에 알맞은 대답을 고르세요.

1. 다음 글에 해당하는 날씨 그림을 고르세요.

   Dark clouds appeared in the sky.
   Soon, it started to rain.
   "It's not sunny at all," Alex said.

   ⓐ **ⓑ**

2. 다음 글에서 them이 가리키는 사람은 누구인가요?

   A drone can help them.
   It checks tall buildings.
   It looks for cracks or other problems.

   ⓐ engineers
   ⓑ firefighters

3. 빈칸에 들어갈 알맞은 문장을 고르세요.

   To stay safe, we follow some rules.
   ________________.
   It protects my head.

   ⓐ I always wear a helmet.
   ⓑ I always stop at a red light.

4. 빈칸에 들어갈 알맞은 단어를 고르세요.

   I was lazy, and I got up late.
   "How about making a daily ________?" Mom says.

   ⓐ party
   ⓑ schedule

Review Test 1 69

p.70

E 필수 패턴을 활용해 우리말에 알맞은 영어 문장을 완성하세요.

How about ____?	It can help ____.
It's fun to ____.	Watch out for ____!

1. 나무를 심는 게 어때?
   → **How about** planting a tree?
2. 공을 차는 것은 재미있어요.
   → **It's fun to** kick a ball.
3. 바위들을 조심해!
   → **Watch out for** rocks!
4. 그것은 경찰관들을 도울 수 있어요.
   → **It can help** police officers.

F 우리말에 알맞은 영어 문장을 쓰세요.

1. 하루 종일 눈이 올 거예요. (be, snowy, it'll, all day)
   → **It'll be snowy all day**.
2. 나는 내 숙제를 끝내려고 노력했어요. (tried to, my homework, I, finish)
   → **I tried to finish my homework**.
3. 우리는 플라스틱을 재활용해야 해요. (plastic, recycle, we, have to)
   → **We have to recycle plastic**.

70

p.127

Review Test 2
(Unit ⑤ - Unit ⑧) / 25개

A 그림에 알맞은 단어를 고르세요.

1. ⓐ call ⓑ grow **ⓒ fight**
2. ⓐ decide ⓑ choose **ⓒ hide**
3. **ⓐ plant** ⓑ hurt ⓒ breathe
4. ⓐ finger **ⓑ straw** ⓒ string
5. ⓐ leaf **ⓑ seed** ⓒ sprout
6. ⓐ movie ⓑ seal **ⓒ sea**

Review Test 2 127

p.128

B 그림을 보고 알맞은 문장을 고르세요.

1. **ⓐ They look at the movie posters.**
   ⓑ They buy some popcorn.
2. ⓐ I was sad to say good-bye.
   ⓑ I found a kitten in my backyard.
3. ⓐ A pumpkin started to grow!
   ⓑ Small flowers came out.
4. ⓐ A plastic bag was stuck on its head.
   ⓑ It got tangled in a fishing net.

★★ **C** 알맞은 단어를 골라 문장을 완성하세요.

1. I can't wait to (**ⓐ grow** ⓑ growing) a big pumpkin!
2. It (ⓐ were **ⓑ was**) hiding in a bush.
3. Emma and her friends (**ⓐ go** ⓑ goes) to the movies.
4. A sharp straw was stuck in a (ⓐ turtle **ⓑ turtle's**) nose.

128

p.129

D 짧은 글을 읽고 질문에 알맞은 대답을 고르세요.

1. 빈칸에 들어갈 알맞은 단어를 고르세요.

   Emma chooses the animal movie.
   "The animals go on a trip together.
   It looks ________," she says.

   ⓐ exciting
   ⓑ sad

2. 빈칸에 들어갈 알맞은 단어를 고르세요.

   Jack planted pumpkin seeds. He watered the seeds every day. A few days later, the ________ sprouted.

   ⓐ seeds ⓑ fruits

3. 밑줄 친 poster에 들어갈 알맞은 제목을 고르세요.

   I found a kitten in my backyard.
   I made a poster to help the lost kitten.
   I put it up at the park.

   ⓐ That's My Kitten!
   ⓑ Is This Your Cat?

4. 빈칸에 들어갈 알맞은 문장을 고르세요.

   ____
   Then, sea animals can live safely.
   Let's help keep the sea clean!

   ⓐ We must not throw trash into the sea.
   ⓑ We must not use plastic.

Review Test 2 129

p.130

E 필수 패턴을 활용해 우리말에 알맞은 영어 문장을 완성하세요.

I can't wait to ____!	It was time to ____.
They talk about ____.	We must not ____.

1. 개에게 먹이를 줄 시간이었어요.
   → **It was time to** feed the dog.
2. 그들은 어느 버스를 탈지에 대해 이야기해요.
   → **They talk about** which bus to take.
3. 눈사람을 만드는 게 너무 기다려져요!
   → **I can't wait to** make a snowman!
4. 우리는 물을 낭비하면 안 돼요.
   → **We must not** waste water.

F 우리말에 알맞은 영어 문장을 쓰세요.

1. 말하는 앵무새들이 있어요. (are, parrots, talking, there)
   → **There are talking parrots**.
2. 그것은 빠르게 움직일 수 없었어요. (fast, move, couldn't, it)
   → **It couldn't move fast**.
3. 나는 경기에서 져서 슬펐어요. (was, the game, I, sad, to lose)
   → **I was sad to lose the game**.

130